JEHOL
CITY OF EMPERORS

JEHOL
CITY OF EMPERORS

BY

SVEN HEDIN

AUTHOR OF "ACROSS THE GOBI DESERT" ETC.

Translated from the Swedish by

E. G. NASH

GYAN

Published by

Gyan Publishing House
5, Ansari Road
Daryaganj, New Delhi-110002
Phone: 011-47034999, 9811692060
E-mail: books@gyanbooks.com

Distribution Network
gyanbooks.com
India, USA, Canada, UK, Australia, France

ISBN : 978-81-212-22365-2 (PB)
First Published, 1932

2nd Impression 2021

Printed at: Gyan Press, Delhi.

Jehol
City of Emperors
Author: Sven Hedin

JEHOL
CITY OF EMPERORS

BY

SVEN HEDIN

AUTHOR OF "ACROSS THE GOBI DESERT"
ETC.

Translated from the Swedish by
E. G. NASH

LONDON
KEGAN PAUL, TRENCH, TRUBNER & CO. LTD.
BROADWAY HOUSE: 68-74 CARTER LANE, E.C.
1932

The Potala Temple, Jehol, through the centre arch of the *p'ai-lou*

CONTENTS

LIST OF ILLUSTRATIONS

List of Illustrations

List of Illustrations

List of Illustrations

LINE ILLUSTRATIONS

FOREWORD

THIS book would never have been written had not my countryman Mr. Vincent Bendix of Chicago expressed a wish to have a Lama temple—either an original or a replica—erected in Stockholm, and another in Chicago, providing me most generously with the funds necessary for such an enterprise.

Jehol, the summer residence of the great Manchu Emperors, seemed pre-eminently the place for the study of such Lama temples. To pull down and remove one of these pearls of Chinese architecture would have been a piece of vandalism unworthy of westerners, and indeed the Chinese authorities would not have allowed such an act of sacrilege; so we decided to begin by making a replica of the stately Golden Pavilion in Potala (Pl. I) for Chicago, while work on the second replica for Stockholm could wait for a while.

At the moment of writing, the Chicago temple has already reached its chosen destination, together with the innumerable objects of religious ritual which pertain to the furnishing and decoration of the temple halls. The articles—many more than 2,000—destined for the Stockholm temple, are in our ethnographical museum, where they are under the care of Professor Gerhard Lindblom and Dr. Sigvald Linne.

On my visit to Jehol I was accompanied by Dr. Gösta Montell, our ethnographer, and Georg Söderbom, his assistant.

Dr. Montell has taken all the photographs reproduced in this book, and Mr. Söderbom made the sketch map of the Jehol temples. For their faithful and valuable work I now thank them most warmly.

Montell, Söderbom and I are under the deepest obligation to Mr. W. H. Liang, our architect, for his skill, inexhaustible patience, and unvarying kindness, during our work together in Jehol and Peking. Our ethnographical museum, too, owes him a debt of gratitude, for he presented me with a beautifully made and very valuable wooden model of the Golden Pavilion, which I have deposited in the ethnographical section of the Riks Museum in Stockholm. We hope, one day, to have an opportunity of welcoming Mr. Liang to Stockholm, when the time comes for erecting the temple here under his direction.

I also wish to express my thanks to our friend and fellow-worker, the learned sinologue, ethnographer, and student of comparative religion, Professor Ferdinand Lessing, of the Museum für Völkerkunde, in Berlin, who now lives in our Swedish house in Peking, and who provided me with the material, obtained from Chinese sources, in chapters IX–XIII.

Mr. T. K. Koo, Librarian of the National Library in Peking, has translated, with the greatest accuracy, the documents, taken from the original Chinese archives, that are quoted in chapters VII–IX, and I wish to express my warmest thanks to both him and his chief, Dr. Tung Li Yuan.

I have called this book—written in such free time as I had in Peking during the autumn of 1930—*Jehol, City of Emperors*. In reality that title is misleading and not descriptive of the text, for, to tell the truth, the reader will search in vain for any description of that city of monastery-temples which forms a fairy-like curve of sanctuaries north and east of the walled park of the Summer Palace.

I might have called it, with as much accuracy—perhaps more—*Ch'ien-lung, The Son of Heaven*, for the great Manchu Emperor who built the majority of the temples and pavilions in Jehol is the chief character in the book and plays the main rôle in nine of the thirteen chapters.

With the help of fantasy, this book might have been made into a romance concerning the brilliant reign of Ch'ien-lung, but I have preferred to keep to the solid ground of truth. The historic events connected with Jehol have been built up from western sources, and from Chinese documents, scarcely any of which have ever before been translated into western languages. In chapters IX–XII fantasy has a place, and there we are principally indebted to modern Chinese authors. If, in the description of the flight of the Torgot, and the funeral cortège of the Tashi Lama across the whole of Eastern Asia, I seem, to some extent, to have overstepped the boundaries set by the meagre historical records, I have not gone further than my own experience of those districts justifies.

Dr. Montell, who took all the beautiful photographs, and I, who wrote the text, will be only too delighted if some of the magic atmosphere that we felt during our visit to Jehol, the Fontainebleau of China, succeeds in reaching our less romantic climes.

When we have an opportunity of setting out the rich collection of objects, ritual and artistic, belonging to the Lamaist religion, which, thanks to the open-handed generosity of Mr. Vincent Bendix, we were enabled to acquire, this book may serve as a guide and afford some description of the milieu with which the magnificent Lamaist religion has surrounded itself.

In addition to this, Professor Lessing, Dr. Montell, and I have planned to write a series of purely scientific monographs describing Lamaism, its rites, imagery, ceremonial objects, iconography, liturgy, ritual, mythological-legendary texts, and the architecture of its most characteristic temples. Even in this plan we have been aided by Vincent Bendix, and, if we succeed, as I hope we shall, in carrying out our intentions, our countryman in America will have contributed to Swedish study of comparative religion and ethnography in Eastern Asia even more than he has by the gift of two Lama temples. This book is a first step towards our future goal.

STOCKHOLM,

July 18th, 1931. SVEN HEDIN.

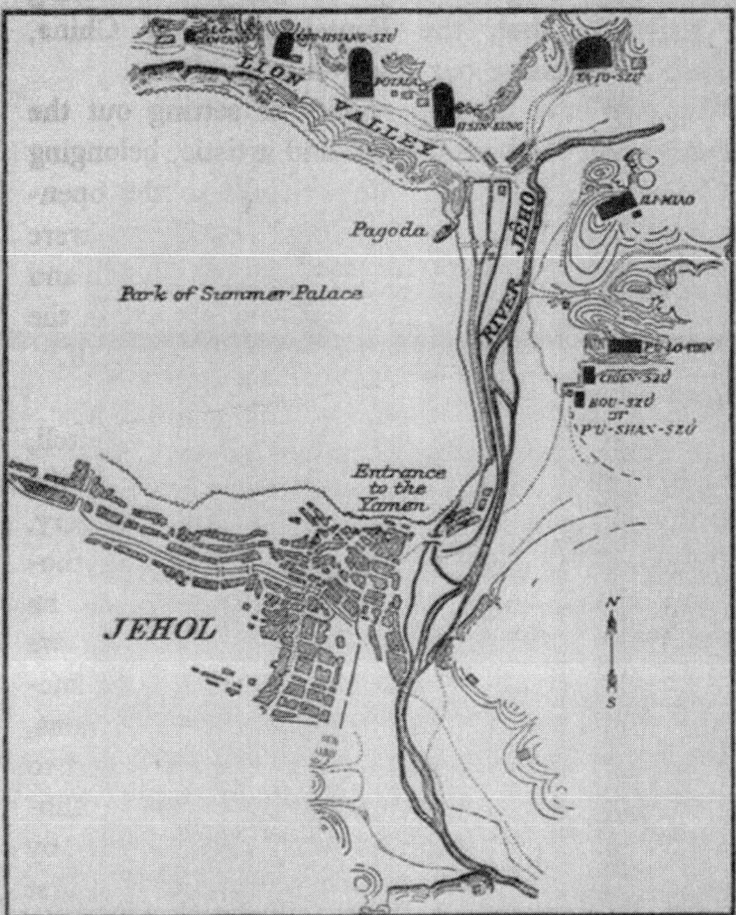

SKETCH MAP OF JEHOL AND ITS MOST IMPORTANT TEMPLES, BY GEORG SÖDERBOM.

JEHOL
CITY OF EMPERORS

CHAPTER I

THE ROAD TO JEHOL

AT last the day arrived when we set off for Jehol, the summer residence of the great Manchu Emperors. A magic city, conjured up out of the Mongolian wilderness at the behest of two autocrats ; a city that, by its incredible riches, its display of imperial pomp and state, its exquisite art treasures and superb buildings, should strike awe into the hearts of the half-wild Mongolian tribes, their khans and their kings. In former times these proud, free-born princes, the descendants of Chingis Khan, riding at the head of their countless hordes of horsemen, had conquered almost the whole of Asia and been a constant menace to the Middle Kingdom. It was worth while building, within the very boundaries of Mongolia, a city that, by its religious character and the splendour of its temple buildings, should serve to bind, with the golden chains of faith and worship, the followers of Lamaism to the Son of Heaven and the Dragon Throne.

So Jehol sprang up, flourished for a hundred years, declined, and was abandoned, died and was forgotten. But Jehol is still rich in memories of historic events and romantic love adventures. Let us listen to the echoes of the past that still whisper among the pleasure pavilions, pagodas, and temples, and to the sighing and murmuring of the wind in the tops of the ancient pine-trees.

It was June 25th, 1930. Since the New Year, our headquarters had been in Peking. Couriers, letters, and telegrams had kept us constantly in touch with the nine expeditions that were working for us in the heart of Asia. Now we too were about to start. The summer was hot and oppressive. In Northern China the rainy season sets in about the middle of June when the roads are turned into seas of mud and it is no easy matter to get a car across the flooded rivers that lie between Peking and Jehol. There was no fear of our being cut off from Peking, for the vast river-road of the Luan-ho would always be available, and, even though its banks were infested with bandits, in the darkness of the night our boat could glide past unseen, on its way to the sea.

Stately weeping-willows hung down over the lilac bushes in the courtyards of our Chinese house in the south-east quarter of the Tartar city. For days there had been the hurry and bustle of departure, but now we were ready. At last! The whole of our equipment, photographic apparatus, sketch-books, and clothing, filled three small chests. The sleeping-bags and a tent were rolled up into two bulky bundles, and our cook, the classic Lü Wu, had packed all his kitchen utensils and provisions in a couple of packing-cases. When all these, and a supply of petrol, had been tied to the running-boards of our Ford, it required no little agility to climb into one's place.

In the back seat sat Dr. Gösta Montell, the head of our ethnographic section, the Mongol chauffeur, Dongora, and Lü Wu ; at the wheel was the irrepressible Georg Söderbom, and I next to him.

At 11 o'clock the engine began to hum and we rolled away through swarms of pilgrims, rickshaws, and carts, and under the huge, imposing An-ting-mên Gate. Crossing the bridge over the town moat, we were soon swaying between the open stalls in the streets of the outer-town, with their noisy chaffering, and colourful crowds of human beings, riders, caravans, jangling bells, and clashing cymbals. Suddenly there was a sound like that of flutes from the air above our heads ; the melodious notes were produced by tame pigeons with little, light pipes attached to their tail feathers.

What strange processions the walls of the An-ting-mên Gate must have seen : emperors' trains, victorious armies with golden dragons writhing across the folds of their banners, brides, bridegrooms, wedding-processions, and the dead, accompanied by priests, relatives, and religious emblems, on their way to the darkness of the grave.

Soon the last house was left behind. We were

going towards the north-east between green, scented maize fields. It was midsummer and delightful to leave Peking with its dirty streets and flying dust. We crossed the well preserved wall which in the days of the Mongol dynasty had been the north wall of Peking that Marco Polo described so marvellously.

Willows cast their shadows over the road. We drove slowly. A *p'ai-lou*, or triumphal-arch, marked the grave of a Manchu prince. From time to time the road led between the grey walls and scattered clumps of trees of a little village, but, for the most part, fields of six-foot-high grain waved and shimmered as far as the eye could see. Very occasionally we passed, or met, rickshaws, and now and again a donkey-caravan taking vegetables or coal to Peking.

Away to the north-east were mountains, lightly etched against the sky. We splashed through a stream and stopped under some shady trees on the opposite bank to sample Lü Wu's provisions. On the grass he spread out chicken, eggs, hors d'œuvres, cakes, and coffee. The countryside was still and silent, and there was not a sign of life. The temperature was 88·7° F. and the midsummer wind was rustling sadly through the tops of the willows and acacias. In olden times this spot had seen the passing of emperors and empresses, carried in yellow palanquins, and accompanied by high mandarins; generals riding at the head of their troops; eunuchs, concubines, and slaves. Now the only splendour on the road to Jehol was that provided by the red afterglow.

We were on the bank of the Pei-ho, the north river that runs into the bay of Chihli at Taku.

It was warm, 95·9° F. in the shade at 4 o'clock in the afternoon. The dust rose in clouds, as two motor-buses came along the road from Jehol. The maize-fields were a rich green ; here and there were cultivated patches of hemp and sunflower ; black goats were grazing on the slopes, and behind the village of Shih-hsia the rocky defile grew so narrow that our bulky car had to be unloaded.

Before the evening shadows had deepened, we pitched camp in an open courtyard in the little village of Pai-ho-chien (The Ravine of the White River). The villagers looked askance at us when they found we preferred to sleep in the tent instead of in one of their simple huts. Certainly a great many Europeans had passed on the road to Jehol, but never before had any of them chosen this poor little village to sleep in.

Gradually darkness fell over the valley, and the head-lights were switched on for us to have supper by. Round us sat the villagers, silent and staring, while thousands of gnats and moths danced about in the bright beams.

The air was cool and the stars peeped in through the tent opening. For a long time I lay awake, listening to the noises of the night. Small caravans of donkeys and creaking carts went past, and one could hear voices talking about the little daily happenings, and certainly about our blue Mongolian tent with its white characters *fu*, the symbol of good fortune, and *shou*, that of longevity. Crickets chirped incessantly; from time to time there was the cry of a night bird, or the far-away barking of a dog—all the well-known noises I had heard for so many years from the coasts of the Mediterranean to those of the Yellow Sea.

The next morning our road led through a narrow, sparsely wooded valley with flocks of grazing sheep. On a low *karnis* we followed the course of a little stream. At last the road was nothing but an unbroken succession of sills and terraces in the rock itself. We swayed as if we were on a choppy sea, and were thrown helplessly to and fro as we tried to protect ourselves from the worst bumps. In the narrow defiles our boxes and tins were badly scratched, but the country was idyllic.

We went through a little village in a clearing surrounded by fields of ripening grain. Hooting furiously, another car kept close at our heels, and at the next clearing it passed us carrying a crowd of yelling soldiers. They ought not to have been in such a hurry on the worst motor-road in the world, and a little farther on we found them stuck fast with a broken axle.

Clear streams ran beneath ruined stone bridges. The valley opened, and on the hills we could see old watch-towers. Some travellers had thrown themselves down under the shadow of a straw roof, in a clump of trees where a little tea-house invited one to rest.

Once again we sped through a village street where black pigs were rooting. The houses were covered with prismatic roofs of straw or tiles. Here they cultivated millet and *gao-liang*, the principal seed-crop of Manchuria. Suddenly, in the midst of the rocky defile, we came upon a little temple with a gateway across the road ; on the other side the ground fell straight away in a hair-raising series of stone sills. The place was called Nan-t'ien-mên (The South Gate of Heaven).

Splendid mules and strong donkeys passed with their burden, and sure-footed boys trotted along carrying their belongings in baskets hung from the ends of bamboo poles which jerked up and down in time to their springy steps.

Leaving one more little village behind us, we came out into a broad, open river valley of gravel and sand. The river was the Chao-ho, a tributary of the Pei-ho. There was a fortification on the top of one of the hills. The ferry-boat was too small for our car, so our baggage was carried across. Thick and yellow as pea-soup, the water slid quickly over the river-bed ; the depth was only about two feet, while the breadth was a little more than fifty yards. The lightened car moved out into the river, where the water got into its magneto, and there it stuck, in the middle of the rushing stream, until the ferry-coolies pushed it across.

On the other side, the road led up through a narrow defile in a valley, and after a while we were in Ku-pei-k'ou, a town situated beside the Great Wall, on the border between the provinces of Hopei and Jehol, and noteworthy as being the beginning of the "Emperor's Road" which leads over Mongolian territory to the Summer Palace in Jehol.

On both sides of the valley the Great Wall wound its way over the tops of the ridges, and, to the right and left of the road, it was crowned with watch-towers like truncated pyramids. Between grey block-towers a steep street led up into the town, while upon the gate itself was a temple decorated with two stone dragons. Here the houses were roofed with black tiles, and white and blue sun-blinds were stretched above the open stalls, where red apricots lay piled up in heaps.

So we swayed and bounced through Ho-p'ing-mên, where the river swirled at the foot of the wall. The military outpost at the gate made no attempt to stop us, and no customs officer asked impudent questions about our baggage, yet we were on the border between China and Manchuria, for the province of Jehol is now included in Marshal Chang Hsueh-liang's realm —"The Three Eastern Provinces" (Heilungkiang, Kirin and Mukden).

In this district the Great Wall is built of dressed stones below and of dark bricks above. The Ho-p'ing-mên Gate is shut at night, and in this way communication between China and Manchuria is cut off.

The next rock defile was unpleasantly steep and

1. The Golden Pavilion (p. xi)

II. An old *p'ai-lou* at the entrance to Jehol (p. 13)

narrow, and we had to drive very carefully in order not to risk breaking a spring or a back-axle. The view over the river winding along far below was magnificent. New watch-towers appeared crowning brown-grey mountains whose slopes were dotted with green bushes and tussocks.

We crossed a series of sills and outcrops, separated from one another by level, earth-covered stretches. On one of these, among other crops, opium-poppies were being cultivated. In the river-beds the car forced its way with difficulty through the gravel and sand ; as yet there was no sign of the approach of the rainy season. The weather was beautiful ; at 1 o'clock the temperature was 91·4° F.

At the village of Liang-chien-fang we stopped for a time to look at all that remains of an Imperial Rest-house. Surrounded by tall pine-trees lay broken walls, gables, and heaps of gravel, the ruins of a fairy castle where the Son of Heaven used to rest on his way to Jehol.

A more idyllic spot for a rest-house could hardly be found. Over a watercourse in a side valley there had been a bridge of which only the stone foundations remained. Yet only seventy years have passed since the last Emperor travelled up this road, and it is astonishing that the bridge should have become so completely ruined.

While we were eating lunch in the shade of a pine-tree a couple of herdsmen came by driving a herd of horned cattle through the valley. The men had long, slightly bent, three-pronged spears, and with them they picked up small stones or lumps of earth, which they flung, with unerring aim, at any of the animals who strayed from the right path.

The valley narrowed and on the left rose a precipitous wall of cliff. Shut in by the mountains lay a little village. We had to drive very carefully over that appalling road, which was nothing more or less than a dangerous, outward-sloping shelf; at last it led straight down to a dried-up watercourse between great boulders. There we could stop and reconnoitre the ground. With all our united strength, we rolled aside some of the boulders in the middle of the road, and filled up the holes between those we could not remove. Then we drove on a little way.

The car lurched and swayed and groaned, every now and again scraping its bottom against rocks that cropped up in the road. A little farther on we stuck so fast that the wheels had to be lifted with the jack and stones placed underneath them. We had met two motor-buses. How in the world do they manage on that astounding road? The passengers have to get out and the chauffeur drives on till the car is a wreck.

In Dzungaria the roads were miserable enough, but not so bad as that between the two Imperial cities, Peking and Jehol. It was fortunate for the Son of Heaven that he was wafted in a palanquin over the terraces and boulders of the Emperor's Road.

We had unloaded every ounce to enable us to get

over that difficult stretch; now, while the others stayed with the baggage, Söderbom and I drove on. Like a clockwork goat, the car climbed up the sills and terraces and bounced over the boulders; we had to hold fast in order not to be pounded to a jelly. To the left of the road, at the foot of a precipitous hill of solid conglomerate, was a miniature temple, with steps leading up to an open balcony supported by four wooden pillars. After we had reconnoitred the ground and found that the road up to the top of the hill could only be safely negotiated in daylight, and as dusk was beginning to cast its shadows over the mountains, we decided to spend the night on that balcony. Söderbom fetched the others, and, by dark, we were comfortably installed under the protection of the silent gods.

By the light of a lantern we ate our evening meal, and then slept splendidly on the stone floor. Some soldiers came and peered at us, and assured us that they would clear the road of bandits and highwaymen so that we could rest in peace.

The next morning we breakfasted beside a little votive shrine under the shade of a pine-tree in the village of Wang-chia-ying-tzŭ (Wang's farm). A villager provided us with hot water for our coffee, and a small naked boy sat and puffed the charcoal into a glow.

Soon we reached the Luan-ho, and easily crossed its first two shallow branches. The car was taken in the ferry over the third one, which is broad and swift.

At the moment the greater part of the river-bed was dry, but after heavy rain it can rise to gigantic proportions. On the other side, the road between the mountains was soft. To the right towered a cliff that erosion had formed into two columns, with a narrow opening between them. Then there was a pass between steep stony slopes and, after that, a ravine with dangerous precipices, and stretches of wild scenery.

Now we had only a few more *li* [1] of the worst motor-road in the world. It was almost impossible to believe that this was the same road about which Hüttner, a member of Lord Macartney's embassy, wrote, only 140 years ago:

> "The Emperor's Road from Peking to Jehol is 418 *li* long, or 22 German miles, and is fully repaired twice a year. It runs right through the main traffic route, and is ten feet broad, a foot high, and made of a mixture of sand and clay, so evenly damped and so well packed that it becomes as hard as cement. That Emperor's Road is as clean and as smooth as the floor in one of our drawing-rooms. It is constantly swept, not only to remove fallen leaves, but the smallest grain of dust. On either side there are reservoirs, every 200 paces, from whence—often with great trouble—water is carried for damping the road. Probably in the whole world there is not a more beautiful road than this one, when it has been cleaned in readiness for the Emperor's journey to Tartary. Watch-posts are set up along the road and no one is allowed to step on it until the Emperor has passed."

Now we could see the famous town.

[1] A Chinese mile, equal to rather more than one-third of an English mile. (Translator's note.)

The road became a street. There were trees; rickshaws appeared, and the houses and shops were closer and closer together. We passed one *p'ai-lou*, and then another, and a yamen, with posted sentries. We drove over a stone bridge, and under still another pair of decorative triumphal arches. A bridge in the middle of the town lacked a parapet and was scarcely wide enough to take the car. Gay shops with many coloured sign-boards; stalls that tempted one to sketch them and their gesticulating customers; narrow alleys, teeming with pilgrims; soldiers; playing children; lazy dogs; small blue Peking carts; donkey caravans; horsemen, and yelling itinerant merchants (Pl. II).

At last we turned to the right into a short lane and stopped at a door where a distinguished gentleman, with mobile features, lively eyes behind spectacles, and a silvery beard, made us heartily welcome in French.

We had covered 114 miles from Peking, and the door before which we drew up was that of the Belgian Catholic Mission; the stately gentleman in Chinese dress who had received us so kindly, was its head, Father Joseph Mullie.

The town which we had reached, where we were to spend ten unforgettable days, was Jehol, the glorious, the Emperor's City, of which the Abbé Grosier, writing over a hundred years ago, said:

> "The most delightful part of all Mongolia is the district of Harchin, which borders on the Great Wall. There the

Emperor goes every year to take his pleasure, hunting, and there he generally spends the whole of the summer.

"In that district he possesses many pleasure-palaces, of which the most wonderful is Jehol. That town, which was formerly nothing but an unknown part of Tartary, has K'ang-hsi to thank for the beginning of its renown. Since the days of that monarch the town has grown without cessation and the embellishments it has received from the later Emperors, the palaces, and the gardens they have laid out, have made a visit to Jehol a delight, especially in the worst summer heat. As a missionary has said, 'Jehol is China's Fontainebleau.' The town is situated in a fertile valley winding among moderately high mountains and watered by a fairly large river, which at times, especially after rains and thaws, can swell to such an enormous extent that it becomes a stream impossible to enclose in any dams."[1]

[1] *De la Chine, ou description générale de cet empire*, Tome Premier (Paris, 1818), p. 272.

Chapter II

THE POTALA

Father Mullie, friendly and affable, led us across the courtyards of the Mission till we reached the innermost one. On the left was the little church, and on the right the guest-rooms, with a dining-room and kitchen ; while directly opposite the entrance-gate was the building where the Father had his own private rooms. The courtyard was charming, with its fine age-old acacias and bright beds of flowers between the stone-paved paths.

T'ien-chu-t'ang (The Catholic Mission) has thirty converts ; and Father Mullie is not only their spiritual guide but a sinologue of vast and profound learning. The great work on the Chinese language which, after many years of sedulous work, he has at last completed, is about to be published in an English edition. In his study, the walls were hidden behind crowded book-shelves. Great piles of books, papers, and manuscripts covered the writing-table, while chairs and small tables groaned under philological works and writings. The atmosphere was weighty with learning ; it smelt of old books and dusty archives, and Father Mullie himself was a sight for the gods as he sat, his yard-long pipe in his hand, poring over some philological problem.

Father Mullie is an ornament to the Mission to which he belongs and he brings still added glory to it by his fame in that branch of knowledge which he has embraced with such enthusiasm. In the autumn of 1930 he was called home to be a professor of sinology within his Order.

On June 28th, our first day in Jehol, Father Mullie took us to the real goal of our pilgrimage, the Potala Temple.

We drove through a labyrinth of narrow alleys and over small stone bridges. On our left we passed the main gate of the park of the Imperial Summer Palace, where the Governor, General T'ang Yü-lin, now lives in the apartments formerly reserved for the Son of Heaven and his court. Above the gate hung the flags of the Republic, and soldiers were on guard. Immediately opposite that entrance to the *yamen*, a stone bridge spanned the Jehol river.

Our road led north, between two well-preserved walls, the one on the left surrounding the Summer Palace park, the one on the right built as a protection against the great Jehol river, which is a tributary of the Luan-ho ; otherwise, after heavy rains, the flood-water would cover the road and cut off communication between the town and the temple, and even threaten Jehol itself.

Inside the Palace wall, quite close to the road, rose a pagoda visible from every direction.

III. The east gate-house in the Potala wall (p. 17)

IV. The Potala: the east gate-house and a dormitory (p. 18)

V. The Potala: Monastery-temple buildings

VI. The Potala: a *p'ai-lou* with five *stupas* on the roof (p. 19)

VII. The Potala: one of the two stone elephants (p. 19)

VIII. The Potala: Elephant Courtyard (p. 19)

IX. The Potala: a dormitory (p. 20)

X. A *p'ai-lou* on the road to the Potala (p. 20)

THE POTALA

A stately marble bridge led over the Lion Valley, and in a few moments we stopped before the eastern gate in the wall surrounding the Potala temple-monastery (Pl. III).

Of this magnificent temple, whose full name is P'u-t'o-tsung-chêng-miao, or Temple of P'u-t'o's Teaching, the Emperor Ch'ien-lung himself writes in the archives, in four languages—Manchu, Chinese, Mongolian, and Tibetan :

> " North of the Summer Palace lies the Potala, which was built not after the Potala on the Southern Sea, but after the Tibetan Potala.[1]
>
> " The Tibetan Potala, ' Du-khang ' (the temple), is complete in all respects and a religious centre for our vassals.
>
> " In the year Kêng-yin (1770) our 60th birthday fell, and, in the year Hsin-mao (1771) the 80th birthday of our August Mother, the Dowager Empress. The loyal Princes from Mongolia and Sinkiang, etc., and the Chiefs of the Dzungar tribes, who had recently sworn allegiance to us, gathered together to bring us their good wishes. As a sign of our encouragement and friendliness towards them we had already begun to build this temple. It was begun in the 32nd year of Ch'ien-lung (1767), and completed in the 8th month of the 36th year (September, 1771). The labour required was great, the temple-rooms are large and everything is dignified and clean in accordance with the precepts.
>
> " Our vassals over the border all believe in the religion

[1] By the Southern Sea is meant the China Sea where, not far from Ning-po, in Chêkiang, there was another Potala, on the island of P'u-t'u. This record has been translated for me by Mr. T. K. Koo of the National Library in Peking, from *A Handbook of Jehol*, Vol. 2, Chap. 19, pp. 33–5. There is no detailed description. Professor O. Franke says, of the Potala, and Hsin-kung, that, as far as he knows, they have not their equal in the whole of China. *Beschreibung des Jehol-Gebietes* (Leipzig, 1902).

of Sâkyamuni. Jehol was the spot where our grandfather, the Emperor K'ang-hsi, pacified and appeased them, and there he granted them audiences. . . . Now the temple is finished in time for a great national event that is to be celebrated by all, in a unique manner. In addition to this, the Torgot, who have lived in Russia for some time, have returned, for religious reasons. The whole of their tribe —which numbers many ten-thousands—arrived just at this time, after wandering about for more than six months. Here is a coincidence that is mystic."

Even at the first glance the Potala impressed us as being vast and imposing to a degree. Certainly its splendour was tarnished; the numerous temples bore the impress of decay, and many of the pines and firs in the temple park had fallen to the axes of impious soldiers. But the grandiose architecture, the vast dimensions, and the consummate elegance still remained, and we stood amazed before that noblest of religious monuments from the last period of China's greatness.

To the south was the main gate, with its three arches, surmounted by a decorative wooden tower, or gate-house, and, to the east and west, were the walls which surrounded the whole group of buildings. These too had gates in them, but they had only one arch. We entered the temple-park through the east gate, above which was a gate-house with a gracefully curved roof covered with shining yellow tiles. (Pls. III and IV.)

We wandered slowly westward among scattered pines and firs towards a building that shimmered in delightful shades of yellow and pink, a *p'ai-lou* with three archways and five *stupas* of the pagoda-shaped, Tibetan type, for holding relics, on the roof. (Pl. VI.)

Through this *p'ai-lou* we entered a little square courtyard, where, under shady trees, two superbly carved, life-size stone elephants kept guard over the entrance to a massive stone building which contained the Potala memorial tablets, or archives, engraved in four languages on three immense, vertical blocks of highly polished stone. (Pls. VI and VII.) Among other records was that of the Emperor Ch'ien-lung quoted above, concerning the three joyous reasons for the building of the temple. The pavilion of the archives was a square building, raised upon a stone terrace, surrounded by a gracefully carved marble balcony. Four open arches led into it, and through them blew, unhindered, the summer winds and the winter blizzards. The roof was double, and had suffered badly from the weather, while weeds and bushes had found a footing between the cylindrical tiles. They had been forced apart; the rain had seeped in, and the woodwork was badly rotted. (Pl. VIII.)

The Potala temple-monastery was on the southern slope of a hill bordered on the north by the Lion Valley. So, when we walked northward through the scattered clumps of pines, we went up shallow steps of undressed stone, just as in Tibetan monasteries.

In the background rose the grand, heaven-storming façade of the Potala itself. First we passed through a *p'ai-lou*, richly ornamented with bright green and red faience, with three archways, and three small, gracefully shaped roofs. Beneath the outer ones were tablets of yellow faience, with flames and writhing dragons in high relief. In front of the *p'ai-lou* two imposing stone lions kept watch. In former times it was forbidden for the *profanum vulgus* to go farther than this *p'ai-lou*; only the monks and the Emperor himself might go as far as the holy of holies, but now all barriers have been torn down and all reverence for holiness is dead.

Between scattered buildings, all with blind-windows, built in the Tibetan style, we went up more roughly hewn steps to still higher places; here the path wound between two bigger stone houses, each with five *chortens* on the roof (Pl. IX). They had been the dormitories and living-quarters of the eight hundred lamas who in the time of Ch'ien-lung served the Potala. Other buildings had been used for common-rooms, class-rooms for the novices, guest-houses for the pilgrims, tea-rooms, and kitchens. To a great extent the rule of the monastery had been the same as it is in Tibet and Mongolia. According to Father van Obbergen, in 1911 there were still 600 lamas, but now there are said to be only 100 monks at the Potala. We saw only a few, as most of them were away in the country round about, earning their bread ministering among the nomads. Those who followed us were shabby and down at heel and lived on the state dole of 1.80 Mexican dollars a month. How can they live on such starvation wages? No longer can they clothe themselves in the prescribed robes of deep red, and no outward sign distinguishes them from ordinary beggars. No one troubles about them now. No one offers them a farthing towards the upkeep of China's most glorious and monumental relic of antiquity. In ten or twenty years it will be nothing but a mass of ruins.

Now we had reached the famous buildings that claim to bear some resemblance to the residence of the Dalai Lama on the Potala hill in Lhasa. The main building was a massive square block, with the façade towards the south. Every other window in the three upper stories was blind, and served as part of the decoration; in the centre of the façade was a row of niches, one above the other, ornately decorated, with miniature projecting roofs, and architraves of glazed tiles, in the elaborate Tibetan style. In every niche was a little image of Buddha, in a sitting position (Pl. XV), and at the top, under the eaves, a row of thirty-four smaller niches, all with Buddhas (Pls. XI and XII).

In certain respects this magnificent façade reminded me of the Royal Palace at Stockholm; there were the same straight, dignified lines and the same vast expanse of wall. But within those mighty walls were no big, light rooms or imposing temple halls, only on the upper floors were there real rooms, with windows looking over the Lion Valley. That gigantic, square block of masonry was nothing but a shell, a decorative erection built round the most sumptuous sanctuary in the Potala, the wooden temple, a faithful copy of which we were to send to the New World.

For some distance up, the walls of this massive shell were built of stone, then they were continued in brick. It stood on a terrace which formed an open, stone-paved courtyard. As our illustrations show, the other monastery blocks were more or less closely connected with this main building. The walls were not absolutely vertical, but leant inwards at a slight angle, so that each block formed a truncated pyramid—just as in the Tibetan monasteries. (Pls. XIII and XIV.)

One hundred and three steps led up to this terrace, from the stone-paved square of which rose the façade of the main building. Here stood an incense-burner and six immense iron bowls which collected the rain-water from the spouts on the roof. Formerly five pagodas, in Chinese style, added to the beauty of the temple, but only two still defy the teeth of time.

On the west side of the balcony-courtyard there was a smaller building with a façade of grey faience, badly damaged by the weather and the encroaching plants. It contained one of Ch'ien-lung's stone tablets, "The Thousand Eulogies of Buddha", dated his 35th year (1770).

Everywhere, between the stones of the terraces, walls, parapets and roofs, grew weeds, bushes, and small trees—the cruellest enemies of the stately monument. Here a botanist should be able to make a very respectable collection. In one room of a side building whose roof had fallen in, there flourished an impenetrable thicket of plants and bushes; wild vines throve, sheltered from all the winds of heaven as though in a hot-house.

There were still three great flights of steps, fifty-nine in all, before we reached the third and highest terrace. It was a square, shut in on all sides by the palace-like mass of the main building which rose three stories high above the courtyard. To-day this wall round the courtyard is a mere shell in which the crumbling, weather-beaten window openings gape; but in former days, inside the walls, there were galleries, rooms, and small temple halls, with innumerable little Buddhas in niches, and possibly, living-rooms for the serving monks. Now the galleries have gone; only the framework of beams remains in one of the corners to show what it originally looked like. (Pls. XVII and XVIII.)

For us this courtyard had a special interest, for in its midst rose the Lama temple, which was the most sumptuous, not only in Jehol, but in the whole of China. It was a replica of this temple which was to be set up in one of the parks in Chicago. When the original has rotted away, the Western World will be able to rejoice that a faithful copy of it has been preserved.

With what excitement we reached the noble goal of our pilgrimage, and, indeed, when we entered the courtyard, and saw that pearl of Chinese architecture, we were seized with admiration and astonishment.

All four sides were alike, and the entrance, which was opposite the altar and the more stately gods, faced towards the south. The double roofs were covered with sheet copper, gilded with dull gold. Their corners curved upwards, a characteristic of Chinese roof architecture, which gave the building a uniquely rhythmic, billowing charm. (Pls. I, XVII, and XVIII.)

The temple was raised on a stone terrace about four feet high, which was surrounded by a stone-paved, sunken walk from which short flights of five steps led up to the middle of the terrace on each side. An open, pillared colonnade ran round the temple, its twenty-eight round, red pillars supporting the lower roof. The upper roof was supported by twelve columns, each thirty-six feet high, rising from the interior of the temple itself. There were, in all, sixty columns of which twenty were affixed to the walls, and the height of the building was sixty feet.

In the interior there was a solemn twilight, which only served to increase the air of mystery that surrounded the gods. What daylight there was, came in by the open doors and filtered through the fretted windows. The altar stood out like a platform. There, throned in Lamaistic majesty, stood a bronze-gilt figure of Tsong-kha-pa, the Reformer, a contemporary of Tamerlane, and a number of offering bowls and symbolic ritual objects. To the east and west, in front of the soaring columns, shining with dull gold, were other

XI. The massive main buildings of the Potala (p. 21)

XII. The façade of the main building (p. 21)

XIII. The Potala: the Round Tower (p. 22)

XIV. The Potala: East Front (p. 22)

XV. The Potala : a niche with Buddha in the façade of the main building (p. 21)

XVI. The Potala: a view of the Golden Pavilion (p. 23)

XVII. The Potala: all that remains of the galleries round the Golden Pavilion (p. 23)

XVIII. The Potala: one of the two last roof pagodas (p. 23)

representatives of the Lamaist pantheon. Most of them had glittering gold aureoles, richly ornamented with flowers, leaves and tendrils. (Pl. XX.) Such is the most beautiful Lama temple in China. There are monasteries and abbeys in Tibet which are incomparably more imposing, whose walls seem to grow out of the very cliffs whose tops they adorn ; but here, in Jehol's Potala, beauty-loving architects had expressed an autocrat's whim in a temple with a rare nobility of line and masterly proportions. Its colours, carvings and patterns roused our admiration, the walls were covered with red and gold, while upon friezes and capitals glowed other colours. The panels and geometrical patterns on the inner roof glittered with the reddest gold, and their carvings were overwhelmingly rich in detail.

Why had this lovely temple been built in a courtyard surrounded by high walls ? The palace-like stone colossus seemed to serve no other purpose than that of hiding the holy of holies from the eyes of the world, and emphasizing the mysticism of the Golden Pavilion.

In times gone by the only parts of it which had been visible from the outside were the five small wooden pagodas that were built on the top of the walls. Now one could see the only two remaining (Pls. XVIII and XIX), and the golden spire into which merged the four sides of the upper roof. As a matter of fact one had no suspicion of its presence. Only from the sun, moon, and stars had the surrounding walls no secrets, and only the birds of the air could see their reflections in its golden roof.

The courtyard of the holy of holies was so small that we tried in vain to get a photograph of the pavilion in its entirety: even in the farthest corners we were too near. If the sun was high, the shadows of the projecting roof fell across the outer colonnade, and if the morning star was on the horizon, the high surrounding walls threw their dense shadows over everything but the upper roof.

In its new position in the land across the sea, this masterpiece of Chinese architecture will come into its own. There, it will be possible to see it standing alone against a background of leafy trees, and there the sinking sun will make the red colonnades glow like real gold.

In the year 1793, when the English embassy, under Lord Macartney, was received at Jehol, the Potala and all the other Lama temples shone in splendour, meticulously tended and cared for by the monks, at the Emperor's expense. Then the Emperor himself worshipped in the Golden Pavilion. In Staunton's description of the embassy, he tells how Lord Macartney was taking a morning walk in the palace park, when he "met his Imperial Majesty who stopped to receive the Embassador's salutations and to tell him that he was going to his devotions in the temple of Poo-ta-la, that as they did not adore the same gods he would not desire his Excellency to accompany him; but that he had ordered his Ministers to attend him through the gardens."[1]

In 1911, the first year of the Republic, there were still some things of value left in the Golden Pavilion. Father van Obbergen saw the beautiful woven silk hangings behind the altar, which groaned beneath a wealth of offering-bowls, incense-burners, and symbolic articles used in the Lama worship. He flippantly compared this religious exhibition to an antique shop. The famous gold figures of the gods were missing, and he supposed that they were packed away in some chests he saw, but, alas, they had been stolen long before by a mandarin who was in need of money. In one corner of the temple he was shown a saddle, a bow, and a quiver full of arrows, which were said to have belonged to the Emperor Ch'ien-lung, and were carefully preserved as relics.

But he already suspected what was to come: "It is plain that this wonder of the world is doomed to swift annihilation!"[2]

During the first day's wandering through the Potala, Montell had taken some fine photographs and I had made some sketches. All the time we were surrounded by inquisitive soldiers and down-at-heel Lamas. They were delighted to see the temple buildings gradually appearing upon the paper. The soldiers were as poor as the monks. Their pay is

[1] *An Authentic Account of an Embassy from the King of Great Britain to the Emperor of China* (London, 1797), Vol. 2, p. 240.

[2] *Deux Illustres Pagodes Impériales de Jehol*, par le père Ernest van Obbergen des Missions de Scheut . . . *Anthropos* VI (Vienna, 1911).

1½ taels per month, but during the last six months they had had none at all. It was not their duty to watch us and our doings, and, when they had got used to us, their interest soon died.

Our first visit to the Potala had been fruitful. What I had heard and read of Jehol was far surpassed by the reality. The park, with its sighing pine-trees, its gate-houses, pavilions, pagodas, the magnificent stone façades, and the noble temple beneath its golden roof, were all equally fascinating, from whatever point one looked at them. From the terraces and balconies on the various hills, the view over the valley was magnificent. When we stood on the highest point we saw the scattered buildings, pagodas and *chortens* in the park far beneath, and, on the south side of the Lion Valley, the hills, over whose ridges, like a grey curving ribbon, ran the wall of the Summer Palace. To the east-south-east we could see the neighbouring temple buildings of Hsin-kung, which we were soon to visit.

Wherever we went, beneath the gold-shimmering roofs of the temples, or under the sighing pine-trees, we could not escape a feeling of sadness over the transitoriness of everything. Everywhere was ruin and decay. From the upward curved corners of the temple roofs still hung small bronze bells, which tinkled a sad little melody at every passing breeze. So had they rung in the days of the Emperor Ch'ien-lung, and so they rang now, in the new China. Then they rang joyfully for festivals and victories and triumphant years ; now they ring funeral chimes for a vanished greatness.

CHAPTER III

THE FLIGHT OF THE TORGOT

AFTER only four years' work the monastery temple of the Potala was finished in 1771. Scarcely a month before, the Torgot, or Kalmuks—as they were called in Russia—had returned to China. In the record tablets, as we have already seen, the Emperor mentioned this historic event as one of the three joyous happenings that were to be commemorated by the building of the Potala. He writes that: "The Torgot, who have lived in Russia for some time, have returned, for religious reasons."

In the records in Hsin-kung, the Emperor Ch'ien-lung says that one of the reasons for the building of that temple was the reunion of the Torgot tribes with his kingdom.

It is evident that the Emperor attached great importance to this event which, the Jesuits assure us, he reckoned among the most important political events of his long and fortunate reign. It will not be irrelevant if we follow the Torgot on their astounding march of death through Asia.[1]

[1] The sources of my information are: C. F. Koeppen, *Die Lamaische Hierarchie und Kirche* (Berlin, 1859); De Quincey, *The Spanish Military Nun and the Revolt of the Tartars* (Oxford, 1909). De

The Torgot were one of the four Eleut tribes. In the beginning of 1600 they had been driven from their grazing grounds round the Blue Sea or Koko-Nor by the Eastern Mongols; and in 1616 they moved to the banks of the Ural river. With their leaders, and fifty thousand tents, they encamped between that river and the Emba and acknowledged the suzerainty of Russia. From there they continued their wanderings to the lower reaches of the Volga. The fact that they had become Russian subjects did not hinder them from plundering Russian towns, time after time. Their kinsmen stopped at Ili and were the neighbours of the Dzungars. In the year 1761, the young Ubasha, of Torgot princely blood, became Khan of the tribe.

On all sides they were surrounded by Christian and Mohammedan races, but they held fast to their own faith—Lamaism—and paid homage to the Dalai Lama in Lhasa. Envoys and presents were sent to him; people made pilgrimages to Tibet, and the earthly representative of Buddha was consulted in times of need. This faith was one of the reasons for the flight of the Torgot.

De Quincey asserts that the wandering of the Torgot tribe through the steppes of Asia has no counterpart in world history. They set out from a country which obeyed the most powerful Christian

Quincey died in 1859. Koeppen asserts that on certain points his account is fantastic, but for all that, he uses him among his sources of information. Certain additions are my own, and based on personal experiences of life and death on Asiatic routes.

authority and went towards lands which were under the domination of the most strongly heathen autocrats. In the unity of will, and the swiftness with which their resolution was carried out, he traces a driving force reminiscent of the urge that, from time to time, sends the swallows and locusts out on such long mysterious journeys. Neither in fiction nor in history could he have found a more dramatic tapestry of events. It lacked neither individual struggles for power, the changing fate of wars, nor the cogency of religious enthusiasm. The flight of the Torgot can be placed side by side with Cambyses' Egyptian campaign, the younger Cyrus and the retreat of the ten thousand, the expedition of the Romans against the Parthians, and Napoleon's retreat from Moscow. The religious aspect of the flight reminds one in some ways of the wanderings of the Israelites through the desert. In his *Nomadic Wanderings of the Kalmuks*, Bergmann says that the whole tribe joined in a cry of alarm: "Our children shall not be serfs for ever. Let us go to the land where the sun rises!"

No pageant in the world, nor any scene, would be big enough for a drama of such colossal size. The flight of the Torgot reminds one of the great folk-migrations of olden times. It lasted seven months, and, with turnings and twistings, covered some 2,400 miles of steppes and deserts. Against a background of constant rivalry for the leadership of the tribe, there were bloody battles fought daily on several fronts against the Russians, Cossacks, Khirghiz, and

Bashkirs, who pursued and hunted the flying Torgot. Of the tribe that, in the beginning, had numbered seventy thousand tents, with four hundred thousand men, women and children, two-thirds died of privation or perished by the sword. Never resting, they journeyed towards their promised land, with millions of animals—camels, horses, cattle, donkeys, mules, sheep, and goats—baggage-wagons and tents, food, household utensils, weapons and their temple *yurts*, raised to the glory of Buddha.

Ubasha Khan and Tsebek Dorche were second cousins, both of them descendants of Ayuka Khan. In the reign of the Empress Elizabeth of Russia, in January, 1761, Ubasha Khan, then a seventeen-year-old boy, had inherited the leadership. He was a well-meaning, friendly man, weak but honourable and upright. Tsebek Dorche, an ambitious and unscrupulous intriguer, considered that, through his noble descent, he had just as much right to the leadership of the Torgot as Ubasha Khan, and sought a way of removing his kinsman from power. The road to his goal lay through St. Petersburg. About the Volga he spread a rumour that among the Torgot nobility there was a conspiracy to assassinate him, and pretending to fear for his life he fled to Cherkassk with sixty-five tents. From there he entered into negotiations with the Cabinet in St. Petersburg, and finally went himself to the capital. With the help of slanders and promises, he prevailed upon the Russian Government to bestow upon the eight members of

XIX. The goddess Çridevi, Protectress of Lhasa and Tibet (p. 25)

XX. Ritual objects

the Torgot *sarga* (council) a power equal to that of Ubasha Khan. The *sarga* was paid by the Government and was therefore dependent upon it. Tsebek Dorche himself was elected president of the *sarga* and so became as powerful as Ubasha Khan.

He played his cards so well that, when he returned to the Volga, both Ubasha and the tribe received him as a benefactor. The good-hearted Khan had no suspicions.

Tsebek Dorche's first conspiracy was against the very Russian cabinet with which he had just been conspiring. He knew that he was playing a dangerous game, but it was necessary for the next step towards the goal of his ambition. He hated Russia, which had not helped him to the Khanship, and he hated Ubasha, who had taken his place. Even the Torgot nobles, who neither slighted nor mistrusted him, were the object of his aversion. Now, by a blow that was crazy in its dramatic greatness and fearful in the consequences that it brought in its wake, he would be avenged on all of them. He would lead all his folk from Russian soil, and by so doing paralyse the Empress Elizabeth's power over the Torgot. He would lead them to the uninhabited districts round the Ili river, where they would be under the protection of the great Emperor Ch'ien-lung, the patron and friend of Lamaism. During the journey he would find an opportunity of putting Ubasha Khan out of the way.

But how could the removal of a whole tribe be

accomplished without the towns on the Volga—even the whole of Russia—getting to know about it? How could one prevail upon those simple Torgot to leave their old abodes, their tents and grazing grounds and their peaceful life on the banks of the Volga, and set out in the winter for a far-away, unknown land, unless it could be shown them that it was the will of the eternal Buddha—and his earthly representatives—that they should do so?

Now Tsebek Dorche's best, in fact almost his only, friend, was the head Lama of the Torgot—Lobsang Gyaltsan—"the most cunning prelate who ever wore a Lama's tiara". He had a personal interest in the proposed flight, for, by leading the true-believers from the power of the Christian Empress back to a Lamaist land, he would gain the favour of the Dalai Lama.

To win over the Khan himself was not difficult. He was good-natured and credulous, and, in addition, a superstitious and fanatical Lamaist. Both conspirators made use of all the terrors and the revengeful spirits that Lamaism has at its command, to force Ubasha to stand fast by the oaths they extorted from him.

Through special envoys they had sought the advice of the Dalai Lama. The prince of the church had assured them that all would go well if the flight were begun in a year of the Tiger or a year of the Hare. Now, according to the Buddhist calendar, 1770 was a Tiger year, and 1771 a Hare year. If they started in the autumn of 1770, the strength of the Tiger and the quickness of the Hare would assist the fleeing Torgot.

The Khan was a weak-willed tool in the hands of Tsebek Dorche and Lobsang Gyaltsan. The former was by now all-powerful, and the *sarga* his obedient servant.

In St. Petersburg there began to be a feeling in the air that something peculiar was about to happen, and suspicions began to gather round the Khan. To throw dust in the eyes of the Government, Ubasha went to the help of the Russians in the war against the Turks in 1768–9 with thirty thousand of his splendid light and heavy cavalry. He was victorious in several battles.

For some unknown reason he never received any thanks from the Empress Catherine II for his services. Not a single ukase, or order of the day, mentioned his bravery, or that of his men. This brought more grist to the conspirators' mill. The Khan should have been elevated to the rank of a Marshal of Russia, but the Empress did not even deign to thank him. Why stay in a land where they were treated like serfs ?

At last the great day arrived when the fate of a whole nation was to be placed in the balance. Even at the end of December, 1770, the Torgot themselves had no suspicion that their great hour was at hand. Peacefully they grazed their herds on the steppes, as their forefathers had done for more than 150 years ; peacefully they went to rest in their tents, where the fires burnt brightly; peacefully they busied themselves with their daily work and their devotions.

How could the terrible message of revolt and flight be spread among them without the Russians hearing about it, and holding up the plan by force? How could that enormous mass of men, women, and children, with their animals, household goods and weapons, be got on the move in silence?

At the order of the Khan, messengers were sent, on fast horses, early in the morning, to the tents of the Torgot to tell them that their arch-enemies, the Khirghiz and the Bashkirs, had attacked their land. According to ancient custom it was the duty of each family to send a representative to the threatened spot. The rendezvous appointed was a hundred and twenty miles away, but within three days eighty thousand horsemen were there.

Then Tsebek Dorche rose in his stirrups and painted in glowing colours all the ignominies the Torgot had had to suffer and the shameful way in which the Russians had treated them and their religion. The conscription to the Russian military service was increasing from year to year; soon a chain of Russian forts would surround them and subjugate them; their noble sons would be dragged as hostages at the hooves of the Russians' horses. Their herds would be taken from them and they themselves would be compelled to move into the towns and be tradesmen—a calling they utterly despised. Before long they would be a race of serfs, and no more would they be able to talk to their oppressors in the tongue of their forefathers, that of the sword and the spear.

Much of his speech was pure fiction, but it did its work. He fired their spirit and awakened their enthusiasm.

But the greatest thing of all Tsebek Dorche dared not tell them yet—that their flight was to be to the far east—to China. He could only force his lips to utter the word Emba—the tribe must fly to the Emba, and take up strong positions on the east bank of the river, and from there, with bold and manly words, state their case to the Empress Catherine.

After the eighty thousand had been stirred up to boiling point, they galloped, post-haste, back to their tents to make preparations for the rash move.

In their camps were many Russian merchants and representatives of the Government in St. Petersburg. Among the latter was a certain Colonel Kishinskoi, whose duty was to keep a watch on the Torgot and their doings. He was controller, spy and ambassador in one, and the intermediary through whom passed all negotiations between the Russian Government and the Khan. His position, therefore, was influential, but he was vain and idle, despised the Torgot, and insulted their princes.

When rumours of the impending flight began to circulate, and reached his ears, Kishinskoi said openly to Ubasha: "You dare not make such an attempt! I laugh at these rumours, Khan, for you are a bear in chains, and you know it." Supercilious and jeering, the Colonel listened to the talk, while the Torgot completed their preparations undisturbed.

The tents seethed like a giant ant-hill. Folk packed their valuables, clothes, blankets, brocades, silver ornaments, images, and household chattels in wooden chests covered with leather. Harnessed to oxen and covered with protecting arched roofs of straw matting and blankets, the heavy baggage-wagons were driven up and the chests tied securely to them. The bottoms of the wagons were covered with straw and mats. Horsemen galloped in all directions ; everywhere there was a feverish bustle and excitement. It was obvious that the nomads beside the Volga were preparing for a journey, a journey the like of which had scarcely ever been known before in the history of the world.

Beketoff, the governor of Astrakhan, pricked up his ears ; he was an infinitely more far-sighted man than Kishinskoi, and they were rivals and deadly enemies. Through his spies, Beketoff discovered everything. He sent courier after courier to St. Petersburg, warning the authorities that the Torgot were preparing to decamp. The Government sent copies of his reports to Colonel Kishinskoi, who roared with laughter at the timorous Beketoff and declared that he would pawn his head if there were any real ground for alarm. The ministers did not know what to think. Nothing was done ; they had faith in Kishinskoi.

On the 5th of January, 1771, the Torgot started on their march across Asia.

Through his spies, Beketoff was the first to hear of the revolt against the Empress. Throwing himself into his troika, with constant relays of fresh horses, he drove day and night, covering three hundred miles in twenty-four hours, till he reached St. Petersburg. There he demanded an audience with the Empress. This was immediately granted, and he made his report, fully justifying his warnings. One by one, other messages came from the towns and forts along the Volga. His triumph was crowned by an order to seize Kishinskoi, who shortly afterwards died of mortification in prison.

So, in different places, at the same moment, the curtain went up on this mighty drama.

One important position was on the east bank of the Volga, another in Tzar Peter's city, which had been built seventy years before as a defence against Carl XII and the Swedes. Between those two centres was to be heard the dull thunder of troika horses, the horns of couriers, and the clanging of bells; the weather-bitten Muscovites hurrying out, their beards white with rime, with flaming, reeking torches, to light up the bustle of changing horses. Behind the veil of falling snow, we seem to see the mighty Empress, white with rage at her ministers' laxity in letting a whole tribe revolt under the very noses of her trusted servants, and flee beyond the boundaries of Holy Russia, thereby drawing down eternal shame on the house of Romanoff and on the watchful eagles with the crown of the Tzar Peter on their heads.

But the east bank of the Volga was the principal scene of this great drama. It was dawn on the 5th January, 1771. The night had been bitterly cold and, when the sun rose above the steppes, the snow glittered with a myriad diamonds. At intervals of half an hour, twenty thousand women and children climbed up into groaning wagons, creaking sleighs, or on to grunting camels, and set out escorted by armed horsemen. In a few hours two hundred thousand women and children started off on their march to death. As far as the eye could reach, black against the snow, were crawling lines of wagons, sledges, camels, and countless herds of cattle and sheep. When the whole tribe had left its old dwelling-place, some ten thousand horsemen stopped behind to fire and lay waste the houses and farms, and make return impossible. The Torgot burnt their boats. For them there was no way home.

Ubasha Khan himself began the destruction. With a burning torch in his hand he went to his timbered chief's-house and set a light to the beams. For miles around the smoke of countless burning houses rose to heaven. Tsebek Dorche's plan included the burning of all the Russian towns, villages, and churches within reach, and death to every Russian they met. But those evil thoughts were never put into practice. People's minds were soon filled with other things. Why was there no sign of the hundred thousand Torgot from the west bank of the Volga? On the east bank the farms were burning, they ought to have understood the signal. But they never came. Mid-winter, the hardest and most difficult time of the year, had been chosen for the start, so that the western Torgot could cross the Volga on the ice, but for some unknown reason they were never heard of. Was the ice not strong enough to bear their wagons and camels, or were they deterred by the manœuvrings of the Russian army in their neighbourhood? No one knows. Fortunately for them, they stayed by the Volga where their descendants live to this day. But the Eastern Torgot, who were not hindered by the broad river, but rather protected by it from their Russian pursuers, were already on their way towards unspeakable misery. The march they were starting was to be stamped by superhuman sufferings, unequalled in history. Blood and tears ran as copiously, perhaps more so, after the ravages of the Huns and the Avars, or in the lands through which the savage hordes of Chingis Khan and Tamerlane passed, but there, the sufferings of the victims were quickly ended and, before the sun went down, all was over and the lamentations had died away. The agonies of the fleeing Torgot lasted for seven months and increased in severity the farther east they got.

The first halting-place was the Ural river, a distance of some three hundred miles. The Khan had given orders that this stretch should be covered in seven days, for it was important to get as far as possible from their enemies and lessen the danger from a pursuing Russian army. So human beings and animals were hurried to the breaking-point ; horsemen followed the endless columns and urged on the wagons, caravans, and their leaders. Even the dogs were exhausted, and the ravens that waited expectantly swept down on outstretched wings, like black banners above a funeral cortège. The cows ceased to give milk, the sheep died in thousands, the children did not get the nourishment they needed. Whether the wagons drove fast, or whether there was a breakdown, whips whistled through the air, shrill shouts rang out. Forward ! Towards the east, towards safety !

At last they reached the Ural river, and everyone rejoiced at the promise of a rest. Most of the Ural Cossacks were away at their winter fishing on the shores of the Caspian Sea, but there were quite enough left behind. Fort Kulagina, which was on the route of the fleeing Torgot, was called upon to surrender, but the commandant refused. The Torgot had only a few pieces of light field-artillery. On the fifth day of the siege, a troop of Torgot on swift Bactrian camels rode up to the Khan's camp. Their news caused evident unrest and dismay. Soon the rumour spread that, the day before, a large body of Cossacks had fallen upon one of Ubasha's detachments, a *uloss*, or clan, called the Feka Tsekhor, and slaughtered them down to the last man. Thus the Torgot lost nine thousand of their best fighting men. No quarter had been asked, and none had been given. For a long time the Cossacks had had a feud with the Feka Tsekhor, now by striking this blow at the fleeing

Torgot they were serving their gracious Empress. The clan had been on the outer flank of one wing, about eighty miles from headquarters, and they had not been able to get help. For the sake of their animals and their pasture the Torgot had to march in a wide-spread formation and the concentration of their fighting forces suffered in consequence. When the shadow of night fell over the Kirghiz Steppe, nine thousand bloody corpses lay in the snow. Now the ravens could stop and from every side came wolves, tempted by the smell. The silence of the grave reigned and the stars shone down on pale faces and eyes that had lost their light, even though they still gazed towards that land of their dreams far away in the east.

At last the siege was raised and the trumpets and drums beat for a hurried departure.

The Turgai was the next river upon whose banks the fugitives hoped to be able to rest and defend themselves against their pursuers, especially the Cossacks who had been encouraged by their victory. On the way they had to cross a pass between hills, a spot where, if the Cossacks reached it first, they could stop their march. Then the Russian troops would be able to fall upon the rear of the fleeing crowds. It was a race between the Torgot and the Cossacks, and the latter had everything on their side, especially their knowledge of the district, and their light cavalry; while the former had their women and children, herds, and wagons. So, instead of lessening the daily marches, as they had hoped to do, they had to increase them.

With horror the women heard what had happened. Some thousands of them now were widows and had lost the protection and help they needed on that terrible journey. They were not even allowed to see their fallen heroes and urged on towards the east; but they understood that it was a matter of life and death for the whole tribe, and that they must stifle their sorrow with still further hardships.

The next day there was a change in the weather. It began to snow, and it went on snowing. Faster and faster fell the flakes; deeper and deeper grew the snow; more and more slowly the long processions struggled through the drifts. White as marble statues, the camels followed in one another's tracks. Snow rose above the axles of the wagons and it grew more and more difficult for the horses, oxen, and camels to draw them along the deeply-cut wheel-tracks. They could not see a stone's throw in front of their eyes and there were no sounds but the creaking of the wagons, shouts of exhortation, and the grunting of the camels.

At last they could get no farther; the going was too heavy, and they had to stop. It snowed without cessation and the exhausted fugitives had to camp for ten days. Even the Cossacks were held up by the blizzard. When the snow stopped there came bitter frost and once again the signal for the march was given. The camels stood the hardship best; they did not feel the cold. Oxen, cows, and sheep fell by the thousand, frozen and exhausted as they were. The winter pasture was hidden under the frozen snow and their leaders saw that the animals that were still alive would not last long; so an order was given that the remaining animals were to be slaughtered and the meat salted and packed in the wagons. For the last time the Torgot could eat their fill, and round the camp-fires they stuffed themselves with meat as never before. No one could rise to any feeling of festivity or hopefulness; there were too many widows. Many a hard-bitten Torgot had left his wife dead or dying by the wayside and countless mothers mourned their children, frozen or starved to death. If they did look forward towards the east, what had they to expect but a misery that would increase from day to day? Already seventy thousand had fallen and, like a black, threatening thunder-cloud in the west, rose the rumour of the Empress' troops who were on the march to strike a death-blow to the fleeing Torgot at the River Turgai.

On the 2nd of February the advance guard of the Torgot reached the narrow defile in the Mukhadsha Mountains, near the river Ishim. Their fears were realized; they found the pass held by the Cossacks.

In this desperate moment, when the safety of the whole tribe hung by a hair, the leader of the Torgot showed courage and resource and, for the time being, even Tsebek Dorche forgot his jealousy and hatred of the Khan. Ubasha threw out a strong detachment of camel-troops against the pass and, when the Cossacks tried to retire, they were cut off by Tsebek Dorche's troops who had crept upon them by ravines and side valleys. When the enemy were hemmed in Ubasha fell upon them with the cream of his cavalry, and a wild and bloody battle surged among the hills. The Cossacks were hewn down to the last man. Thus was vengeance taken for the Feka Tsekhor clan.

Now the road lay open between the Irtish and the Turgai. But behind them the outlook was still black. Spies reported that the governor of Orenburg, General von Traubenberg, with a large army, was marching towards the Turgai. Ten thousand Bashkirs and an equal number of Khirgiz had joined him, mad with religious hatred and thirsting to revenge themselves on those Volga Kalmuks who had helped Russia in the war against the Sultan, the head of Islam, who fought under the green standard of the Prophet.

Once more the daily marches were increased and another race began. They were still some way ahead, but their pursuers had only to follow their tracks. Traubenberg's patrols and spies had merely to report the speed of the fugitives' marches, the number of dead, and the deserted baggage-wagons left behind. Long rows of corpses lay beside the wheel-tracks. The camels were the only support of the fugitives as, with their heads held high, their fixed stately gaze upon the far eastern horizon, they marched steadily on, while around them, human beings died like flies.

Slowly and heavily, the funeral procession passed through the endless steppes. When the sun sank and the winter night came to those dying folk, all longed for the signal to make camp, but it was pitch-dark before the bugles rang out through the icy air. Utterly exhausted, most of them threw themselves down where they were ; the women wrapped their tattered furs closer round the hungry, wailing children ; a baggage-wagon was broken up for fuel, and those who were still able to do so, and had not lain down to sleep and freeze to death, crept up to the fires. When friends and neighbours tried to awaken the sleepers, they were already dead. When dawn broke and the signal for starting sounded, once more the sun shone down upon the steppes, upon a misery beyond the power of words to describe.

Day after day passed, and still the steppes rolled away towards the east, like an endless, billowing sea. The survivors were becoming hardened by the emotional and agonizing scenes that had been repeated time after time—constant farewells to those they loved, those who could go no farther. Some stayed behind to take a last farewell of their dead, after which they would endeavour to catch up the living.

Once more the sun sank, the shadows crept farther and farther across the ground ; it sank in blood, and the whole steppe was red with its afterglow. The heavy baggage-wagons creaked and groaned in wheel-tracks that were deep in slush. The drivers were ten-year-olds, who leant back against the tent bundles, blankets, and leather chests, and slept, while the tired and hungry animals followed in one another's tracks. In every direction were human beings, walking, riding, driving. They went forward on a front several miles broad, or the pasture would not have been enough for the animals. On the flanks rode armed men. In long strings the endless caravans of camels moved forward with slow, measured tread. The evening sun shone red upon them till they looked as if they had been splashed with blood; between their humps sat women, with sleeping, dying children in their arms. No longer did they talk, they merely longed for the next camping place, which many of them would never reach, and which would be the last for many more.

The red, yellow, and green dresses of the Torgot had lost their freshness. They were bleached and tattered and filthy with soot, grease, and blood; the whole once colourful procession had toned down into a universal dusky grey. It was a funeral march through Asia, the most tragic of all migrations.

A young Russian, Weseloff, had been taken prisoner by the Torgot. He has described something of what he saw; the women and children who raised the tents and did the hard work, while the men protected them; but he was closely imprisoned in Ubasha Khan's head-quarters, and could not move about freely among those hordes of poor, doomed folk. Had he been free, and had he possessed the brush of a Vereshchagin, he would not have needed to seek farther for motifs unsurpassed in dramatic grandeur and wild barbaric power.

In red, fur-lined, priestly robes the Lama-monks sat huddled in their saddles, sunk in gloom, mumbling without cessation their prayers and requiems for the dead. Through the constant creaking of the wheels, the squelch of horses' hooves in the trampled mud of the trail, the warning shouts of the drivers, and the grunting of the camels, ran the constant mutter of prayers, the ceaseless invocation *om mani padme hum.* In those days of bitter misfortune the fugitives had more need than ever of the help of the gods, and, in the temple *yurt*, the midnight hours resounded to the blaring of trumpets, the dull thudding of drums, and the clashing of cymbals. But the gods heard them not. Their prayers died away across the endless steppes.

Days, weeks, months crept by, and farther and farther eastwards crawled the procession of death. Winter had passed, the spring had returned, and they had reached a warmer climate. In May the steppes spread their wonderful carpet of blossoms beneath the feet of the fugitives, and, between whitened bones and dried-up skulls, grew anemones and cowslips, beckoning and whispering of life and the joyous return of the sun. Light puffs of air ruffled the grass, and once more the starved animals could graze. At the end of the month the sadly diminished procession crossed the Turgai and took up its position on the east bank of the river. At last they could rest in peace and safety and procure fresh stores from the more fertile tracts. The future looked brighter for the Torgot, but what a price it had cost them to struggle onwards until the spring returned. Five months of cruel suffering and two hundred and fifty thousand dead! The beasts they had lost during their journey were beyond reckoning. Not a single ox, cow, sheep or goat remained, a few horses and mules—only the camels, those ships of the desert, who can always find something to eat among the tussocks and thistles of the steppes, still trod majestically towards the east, where the sun lighted its torch above the wilderness.

Their days of prosperity were gone. Where were the warm huts beside the Volga, where their flocks and herds had cropped the juicy grass of the steppes and meadows, where their children had grown up into strong men and women, and where folk in bright, many-coloured clothes and jingling silver ornaments had gathered for the great temple festivals? Now they were nothing but a crowd of beggars, stripped of their possessions, fugitives who, all unwitting, had given up everything to go towards certain destruction. No. They were a band of heroes, whose faith, patience and endurance are worthy of being remembered throughout the ages.

What were the thoughts of Ubasha Khan as he rode, bent in the saddle, his face set, at the head of these dying legions? He bore the responsibility for the most fateful decision any leader ever took, and he was tortured by qualms of conscience when he saw his brave folk wasting away, since their flocks and herds were swallowed up in the endless steppes. He was responsible for the unutterable sufferings, the unappeasable sorrows, and the lamentations that, daily and hourly, rose to heaven.

But despite his weakness he was courageous and upright. To try and appease his conscience, he called a meeting of the *sarga* and left in their hands the final decision as to whether they should go on, or turn back to the Volga. They could not hope to escape the vengeance of the Empress, but he and he alone would take all the blame ; he would throw himself on the mercy of Russia. No revenge should fall on those innocent folk.

The *sarga* received his message with thankfulness and praised his offer to sacrifice himself for his people.

But Tsebek Dorche threw his whole weight into the balance against the Khan's proposal.

" It is true ", he said, " that pardon would be given us, but no Russian would ever again believe our word. We should be treated with contempt, forts would be built round our land, our freedom would be gone and we should be serfs, while our camps would be filled with secret spies. We have not revolted against Russia, we have only returned to our own land from which we fled a hundred and fifty years ago. To turn back on our trail, to be reminded daily of our intolerable sufferings, to stumble at every step over the skeletons of our comrades, our friends and fellow-countrymen. No, never! We have come eighteen hundred miles and have only three hundred more to China. If we turn back now we shall fall into the arms of the Russian army and the hordes of Khirghiz and Bashkirs. If we hurry towards the east, there is at least a chance that we shall escape from the grip of our enemies. Russia is the land of serfs, China the promised land. So let us go forward—towards the east, towards the east!"

The mass of the tribe, driven to the verge of death, had reached the point of despair. They cursed the day they had left the Volga. Hate and revolt against their leader surged up in the weakening columns. An uproar threatened. The deliberations of the *sarga* reached the ears of the folk, and all of them agreed with the Khan. "Back to the Volga! The Empress will forgive us! We will throw ourselves on her mercy!"

There was wavering and indecision; the uprooted tribe was ground between two millstones—Russia and China—the two greatest empires of the day. They were surrounded on all sides by enemies; they had no permanent city, they raised their *yurts* and lighted their fires in the lands of others, and were strangers wherever they went. Now at the parting of the ways something happened that, in one moment, crushed all their hopes. Another fateful hour had struck for that brave little tribe.

On foam-flecked horses, two riders dashed up to the Khan's head-quarters. They brought a message from General von Traubenberg. He demanded instant and unconditional surrender. There was no alternative.

After a gruelling march, the general and five thousand regular troops had reached the fortress of Orsk in the beginning of June. In May, ten thousand Bashkirs and an equal number of Khirghiz, under the leadership of Nur Ali, had joined him. When these wild hordes of Islam, believing that the Torgot were only ten days' march away, pressed him to push on, he answered that his exhausted troops needed rest. When the leaders of these free Mohammedans, who were burning with hate against the enemies of the Crescent, failed to move the phlegmatic general, they broke away from him, and began, on their own account, to follow in the tracks of the fugitives, making forced marches.

In six days they had reached the Turgai river and swum their horses across. The Torgot had no suspicions. They were scattered over miles of country, watching their camels and looking for food. The Bashkirs fell upon them from several directions. There was fighting and fleeing, and slaughter without mercy. The Khan only escaped capture and death by a hair's breadth. In feverish haste Tsebek Dorche organized a column of picked infantry and a corps of camel troops which he threw against the wings, forcing the Bashkirs to retreat; and, although they suffered dreadful losses, the day was saved.

During the next few days fresh clouds of dust

appeared on the horizon in the west and new bands of enemies grew up out of the steppes. The Torgot hurried their pace, fainting under the burning summer sun, tortured by hunger and thirst. Like smoke from a burning city rose the dust from their horses' hooves, the wagon-wheels, and their camels' feet. The long lines of dusty wagons and camels were silhouetted sharply against the evening sky and slipped like ghosts and shadows through the moonlight. They were too exhausted to weep or lament; they were stupefied with sorrow; the flutes and stringed instruments had been silent for a long time. There was no sound but the dull throbbing of the temple drums at night and the muttering of the Lamas' prayers throughout the long days.

Fresh corpses lay in the wagon tracks and spread a terrible stench. Those who stayed with the dying whom they loved and would not leave, were slain by the Bashkirs. The exhausted ones, who could not go on another step and desired nothing on earth but rest, could not even die in peace because of the sharp teeth of the wolves.

Young Weseloff was still watched, but the farther from Russia they got and the greater their suffering the less careful were his guards. At last the Khan promised him his freedom. Tsebek Dorche maintained that the aristocratic prisoner might serve as a hostage if the Russians took any of the Torgot leaders prisoner. The watch upon him was redoubled. Weseloff complained to the Khan that his holiest feelings were being played with, and Ubasha assured him that it was without his knowledge. To prove his good faith and friendliness he told Weseloff that he had, that very day, received a message from the *hetman* of the Bashkirs asking him to come to a meeting at a certain point on the banks of the Turgai on the following night. The Khan and the *hetman* were each to be accompanied by three men only, and he asked Weseloff to be one of his three.

But the Russian suspected foul play and refused. Besides he had made a secret compact with three Torgot from the west bank of the Volga that they should escape together.

The district teemed with half-wild horses. The Russian and the three Torgot caught some of them and hid them in a forest beside the Turgai. In the night they crept away, mounted their horses and rode off; from different directions they approached an agreed-upon meeting-place. The moon shone down over the silent country. Suddenly a wild cry for help reached their ears and they heard the clash of weapons. Weseloff recognized the Khan's voice. He persuaded the three Torgot to go with him and they spurred towards the spot. In an opening among the trees they saw four horsemen struggling against ten others. Two of the former had already been unhorsed and one of them was fighting for his life against two enemies. Weseloff recognized the Khan, fired, and brought down one of the prince's assailants. The three Torgot fired too, and the enemy, who took them for a whole force of cavalry, turned and fled through the forest.

Weseloff examined the man he had killed, and recognised one of Tsebek Dorche's trusted servants.

Silently they mounted and rode back towards the headquarters of the Torgot. After a while the Khan spoke :

" I understand everything. I ought to keep you a prisoner, but that would be a poor reward for the service you have done me. Do you see that watch-fire ? Follow me there and I shall be in safety. Then go on with your plan of escape. I can repay you in no other way ; but tell me first—did you know of the trap into which I so nearly fell ? "

" No, it was merely by chance that I heard a cry and knew that you were surrounded by assassins, so I hurried to help you."

They reached the watch-fire, and said farewell to one another. The Khan and his escort rode to headquarters, while Weseloff and his three Torgot galloped towards Russia, racing at a mad pace through the corpses and devastation that marked the route of the fugitives. They had stolen a sufficient number of horses to change them constantly. From the Volga, the young Russian continued his way home, where his mother was anxiously awaiting news of his fate. The moment he stepped across the threshold she stretched out her arms towards him, but they fell to her sides and her head sank to her breast. She had borne the endless waiting but the joy of seeing him return was too much for her. She was dead.

What numbers of deep tragedies were enacted during that flight of the Torgot; how many bonds of love and happiness were sundered for ever! What streams of tears and blood flowed on that road of suffering and sorrow, that road whose milestones were hundreds of thousands of open graves, where the bodies were left as food for the wolves and birds of prey. Those who could have told the most heart-rending tales died by the wayside. Those who survived to the end could not bear to be reminded of the nightmare they had lived through. They certainly tried their best to wipe out those scenes of horror from their memories. They would only look resolutely forward to new years of peace and quiet; they would forget their fallen beasts and see new herds grazing on the grass on the banks of the Ili. We are told that many lost their reason and that many others were brooding and melancholy for the rest of their days.

But not yet had the remainder of that dying tribe emptied the cup of its suffering to the dregs. The hardest part of their road still lay before them. The last stage of their death-march far surpassed in suffering anything they had endured up to now.

The summer was blazing hot. There were no trees, not a patch of shade on that endless steppe. Only night brought the solace of coolness. Their stores of food had long since given out. Thousands starved to death and the survivors were consumed with hunger. They went many miles out of their way in order to pass through more fertile districts, and they became like wild beasts who, tortured by hunger, sought for prey. All discipline and order vanished. They became robbers and highwaymen who fell upon villages and camps and plundered everything that was eatable. In the districts they passed through they herded together all the cattle they could lay hands on, slaughtered the beasts where they stood, and ate the raw flesh before it was cold. The men in the ravaged homesteads tried to defend their possessions and there were bloody fights every day. On all the fronts the tortured folk fought for their lives, for the Bashkirs were after them like bloodhounds and gave them no peace.

On the route of the fugitives lay the Steppe of the Yellow Water, a hundred and twenty miles broad. At whatever cost, it had to be crossed. There was water, but it was poisonous and brought on a dysentery-like sickness, with severe hæmorrhage. The yellow water killed still more thousands of Torgot. In that dreadful summer heat they could not resist drinking it. Thirst drove them mad.

At the Turgai river the Khirghiz, who had left the slow Russians behind, had made a detour towards the south, and had now gathered together their hordes on the eastern edge of the Steppe of the Yellow Water. From there, they could hold all the fresh water wells. Starved and exhausted, the fugitives made their way towards the fresh water. Ubasha Khan called up all the columns that were still able to fight and attacked with the rage of despair. Not a man held back: whatever happened they were doomed to death. For two days this terrible battle raged, and streams of blood flowed. Then the Torgot captured the wells, drank their fill and continued their march eastward.

How amazing that they held out! That they did not lie down and die, and be free of an existence that had never given them a minute's peace, only torment, sorrow and death! No, they did not give up. Those dark columns of ragged, sun-burnt folk, with ravaged, bitter faces that had been set by a thousand trials, and had lost the power to smile; those weather-bitten, hard-featured men with piercing, determined glances and clenched teeth, whose fingers convulsively clasped the hilts of their swords and the shafts of their spears. Those long rows of battered baggage-wagons that crept along in clouds of dust; the camels, ragged and grey with dust, but just as majestic as ever; the whole of that swarming crowd who, despite all their detours, still headed east, towards safety on the banks of the Ili.

At last from the tops of the low hills they saw Lake Balkash, its wide, glittering surface spread out before them like a sea. Tortured by thirst, the mass of humanity went crazy at the sight of that clear water. Women of all ages and the young boys who rode the camels kicked their animals into a run and rushed down to the shores. The drivers sprang down from the wagons and followed as fast as their legs would carry them. A dreadful confusion ensued; it was a race to the lake. When they reached the shelving banks they waded into the water up to their knees, up to their waists, and drank and drank. Many drank till they had convulsions and died where they were in the water. The camels, too, waded out to quench their thirst. Fresh crowds rushed down and thrust aside those who were there first. They pushed in among the tightly packed camels, and, when the confusion was at its height, the pursuing Bashkirs and Khirghiz fell upon them. Like blood-thirsty beasts of prey the sons of Islam rushed down into the lake with drawn sabres. To the accompaniment of savage yells they threw themselves into the midst of that mass of people—but they too were thirsty. They killed and drank alternately. The Torgot drew their knives to defend themselves, and, fighting for their lives, Mohammedan and Lamaist sank beneath the reddened water, in a bloody embrace.

The anguished cries of women and children filled the air; the whole place resounded to the wails of the dying. In order to escape from the murderous Mohammedans they waded out till the water reached to their necks, and, with despairing faces, sank to a watery grave in Lake Balkash.

That unholy slaughter would have gone on until not a living soul remained but for an unexpected change in the scene. Among the hills there suddenly appeared more mounted troops. Were they the Russians who had at last caught up their allies and were hurrying to their assistance—to deal the death-blow to the Torgot? No, Chinese cavalry were storming down the slopes. The Khirghiz and the Bashkirs knew that now it was their turn. They lined up their men for defence, but scarcely had they reached the shore when the Chinese artillery opened fire upon their close-packed ranks. A new slaughter followed. The Torgot had a breathing space, at last.

Before the fresh, rested troops of the Chinese the Mohammedans went down like ninepins. They wavered, drew aside, and fled in disorder. The Chinese did not follow them, which, to the Torgot thirsting for revenge, was a pity, but it was a comfort to think that their enemies had hundreds of miles to travel and endless hardships to endure before they reached their own tents.

Lake Balkash was redder than usual in the after-glow of that day's sunset; in the water and on the shore lay thousands of corpses. But when, next morning, the survivors of the tribe heard the signal for the march, their pursuers had disappeared. At last they crossed the river Ili, and were on the other side, in a land that was under the suzerainty of the Middle Kingdom.

Among the many geographical and historical original texts that Mr. Hwang, one of the Chinese members of my expedition, brought along, when we moved from

Peking, in May, 1927,[1] there was one that had been published about a hundred years ago under the title *Mêng-ku Yu-mu-chi*, 'Cattle-breeding and grazing grounds of the Mongols', which bore the names of two authors, Chang Mu and Ho Ch'ui-t'ao. While we were at Etsin-gol, Professor Hsü Ping-ch'ang was kind enough to translate the main facts about the fate of the Torgot.

We are told that the fugitives, in order to escape from their pursuers, took refuge in "Gobi", or the desert, where they could find neither pasture nor water, and that they had to drink the blood of their oxen and horses.

When the governor of Ili, General Shu Ho-tê, received word of their coming, he mobilized a force to defend the border of his province, and sent messengers to ask what the fugitives wanted. Ubasha answered that he was willing to surrender to him, as he and his troops were weary of obeying the Russians, and longed to be back in a Lamaist country.

Four districts were given them to settle in. The first lay north of the Kara-shar, the second east of the Tarbagatai, the third between the rivers Ili and Urumchi, and the fourth east of Kuldja. In addition to this the Emperor gave them 140,000 horses, oxen, and sheep, after they had got 120,000 in Sinkiang. They were given tea, grain, cotton, cloth *yurts*, etc. The Imperial Seals they had received from the Ming Dynasty were to be returned to the

[1] See *Across the Gobi Desert*, Sven Hedin (London, 1931).

Emperor, who, in exchange, gave them new Manchu Seals.

The ancestors of the Torgot our expedition met in Etsin-gol, with whose prince and tribesmen we are still on such a friendly footing, were given dwelling-places near the desert river that was of such strategical importance in the Han and T'ang dynasties, and settled there in the reign of Emperor Yung-chêng.

Since February, 1928, we have been on equally friendly terms with the Kara-shar Torgot and their Prince, Sin Chin Gegen Khan.

The Emperor Ch'ien-lung's expression, both in words and deeds, of his delight over the return of the fugitives, was purely and simply political. The Torgot were the last of the Mongolian races to remain outside his boundaries ; now they had returned to the Middle Kingdom and the dynasty ruled over all the Mongols.

Father Amiot, one of the French Jesuits who visited Peking at that time, was fortunate enough to secure a copy of the text of the inscription that was to be engraved on a memorial stone and, by order of the Emperor, set up on the shores of the Ili river. The original was composed and written by the Emperor himself.

In his preface Amiot says :

> " . . . waiting for history to enlighten posterity on an event which he looks upon as one of the most glorious that happened during his reign, the Emperor had the date and details inscribed on a stone in the four languages—

Manchu, Mongol, Torgot and Chinese—which were spoken by the races under his rule. This stone monument was to be set up on the Ili river, under the eyes of the Torgot themselves, to be within sight of all the nations I have named." [1]

According to Amiot's free translation, among other things, the Emperor wrote the following:

"The Torgot came, and when they came they found dwelling places, food supplies, and all the necessaries that each one needed in his own home. That is not all. The most important among them were invited to come in person and render their homage to me. They were hospitably treated and conducted with all honour along the Emperor's road to the palace where I was. I received them, I talked to them, I was pleased to allow them to join me in the pleasures of the hunt, and when the days that were given up to that open-air life came to an end, they came in my suite to Jehol.

"There I honoured them with a great banquet, and gave them the usual presents, with the same pomp and circumstance that I always employ when I receive Tsering and the chiefs of the Durbets, whose Prince I am.

"It is in Jehol, in that beloved spot, that, having conquered the whole kingdom of the Eleuts, I received the sincere homage of Tsering and the Durbets—the only tribes among the Eleuts who had remained loyal to me.

"Who could have suspected it? When I least of all expected it, when I had not thought of it, just that branch of the Eleut race—that branch that had been the first to cut itself loose, and, of its own free-will, leave its foster-land to go away and live under a strange and distant domination—now those very Torgot had returned of their own accord

[1] *Monument de la Transmigration des Tourgouths des bords de la mer Caspienne, dans l'empire de la Chine. Mémoires concernant l'histoire . . . des Chinois ; par les Missionaries de Pekin.* Tome premier (Paris, MDCCLXXVI), pp. 401 *sqq.*

XXI. The Ili-miao Temple (p. 70)

XXII. The Green Târâ in Ili-miao (p. 71)

XXIII. Interior of the temple-hall in Ili-miao (p. 71)

XXIV. The Tsung-yin-tien pavilion at the P'u-lo-tien temple (p. 72)

XXV. A *stupa* at P'u-lo-tien (p. 73)

XXVI. The temple-hall of Tsung-yin-tien (p. 72)

XXVII. The Round Pavilion at P'u-lo-tien (p. 73)

XXVIII. Interior of P'u-jên-szŭ (p. 74)

to put themselves under my suzerainty. And it happened to be in Jehol—not far from the sanctified spot where the ashes of my glorious grandfather rest—that I, not having striven for this thing, had the opportunity of solemnly receiving them among the rest of my subjects.

" Now the hour has struck when, without fear of exaggeration, one can say that all the races of Mongolia have surrendered to our great dynasty, Ta-ch'ing, and it is true to say that from this dynasty all the Mongolian hordes get their laws. Such was the will of my august grandfather. He had foreseen that it would happen one day. What joy would have filled him if he could have known that that day had at last dawned !

" Scarcely had the Torgot arrived when suspicions were aroused. These people, I was told, are rebels, who fled from the suzerainty of the Russians ; it will not be safe for us to receive them. There is the danger that, if we are friendly towards them, they will prove a source of trouble and unrest within our borders."

Those who entertained these suspicions maintained that, by reason of a solemn treaty between China and Russia, each of the countries was pledged not to receive fugitives from the other, but to send them back at once, or at least punish them ; but to these objections the Emperor replied that he was doing no more than the Russians had done when they received Prince Tsering and the whole of his tribe.

The Emperor continues:

" Do not let this disturb you in the very least," I answered. " Tsering was formerly my vassal ; he revolted and fled to the Russians, and they received him. More than once I ordered them to return him, which they did not do. Seeing his error, Tsering has returned of his own accord and given himself up. What I have said here, I have already told the Russians, down to the last detail, and I have brought them to such a point that they could not answer me.

"How could I, for a reason that I do not even approve, bring myself to let so many thousands of people perish, when they arrived at our border half dead with hunger and misery? People complain that they carried off food and cattle. Maybe they did. How could they have saved their lives if they had not done so? An old proverb says, 'Be so watchful that no one can ever surprise you! Keep such a careful watch that perfect peace reigns—even in your deserts.'

"As for the Ili district where I have allowed them to settle down, despite the fact that I have just had a city built there, it is still a country that is not strong enough to insist on its borders being respected, or to prevent robber bands from plundering it. Its people have no other occupation than that of farming and cattle breeding; how could they defend themselves or keep peace in the desert?"

The Emperor goes on to say that he had been warned in good time of the approach of the Torgot, and he asks what he would have gained by barring their way.

"Would they not—driven to despair—have committed still wilder excesses? . . . would one wish a great monarch, whose first duty is to seek to emulate Heaven in his manner of leading men, to refuse his assistance, and let a whole people who had sought his help be destroyed?

"May such a vile action ever be beneath us! No, we would never use such cruel expedients. The Torgot have come. I have received them. They suffered through the lack of even the most essential means of existence. I have provided them with an abundance of everything. Without food, without clothes, utterly destitute, the Torgot reached Ili. I had foreseen that, and I ordered *Chouhede*[1] and others to have every kind of food in readiness so that they could have immediate succour.

[1] The Governor of Ili, Shu Ho-tê.

"And this was done: land was divided among them and every family was given a certain portion of ground upon which it could support itself, either by cultivating it or grazing its herds upon it. To each one was given enough cloth for clothing, grain for bread to last him a year, household utensils and other necessities, and in addition, several ounces of silver, so that each one could buy anything that might have been forgotten. They have been given a very fertile district for their grazing grounds, and they were given oxen, sheep and other beasts. So that, in time to come, they will be able to work for themselves, support themselves, and take care of their own future."

In one of his letters, Father Amiot speaks about the Emperor Ch'ien-lung's highly trusted minister, Yu Ming-Chung. The latter had spoken of the dreadful misery that prevailed among the fugitives when they arrived, and of the generosity with which they had been received. The Emperor had sent an order to Ubasha, the Khan of the Torgot, to come to Jehol, with his chiefs and other trusty men, and they had obeyed the summons without delay. They were given garments of honour and were received in audience at the Palace of I-mien-yü, situated in the Garden of Ten Thousand Trees; overwhelmed with gifts and titles and given banquets of honour.

The minister says:

"The year that the Torgot returned was the same year that the Emperor celebrated his mother's eightieth birthday. In memory of that happy day, his Majesty had had built on Pi-shu-shan (The mountain that shades from the heat), a large and magnificent 'miao', a temple in honour of all Fo's (Buddha's) Attributes, united under one and the same cult. It had just been completed when Ubasha and the other princes of his tribe came to Jehol.

" To the memory of an episode that contributed towards making that year famous in our annals, the Emperor wished to erect a monument in the above-mentioned temple that would perpetuate this historic event, and vouch for its authenticity."

That temple was the Potala, in the proud construction of which Emperor Ch'ien-lung had immortalized the memory of the flight of the Torgot and their return to the Middle Kingdom.

If the chief Temple in Jehol—The Yellow Pavilion—is doomed to fall into ruins and disappear, its replica, faithful in every detail, will stand on the shores of a lake in North America.

That temple will be cared for and honoured. It will stand in a place of honour as a monument commemorating a feat which, in its greatness, is without equal among human destinies and hazards. Not in inquisitive curiosity will Westerners step across its threshold, but lost in honour and admiration at a people who, with a courage and suffering that were epic, fought their way through the desert wastes of Asia.

Chapter IV

THE HSIN-KUNG TEMPLE-MONASTERY

A DESCRIPTION of all the temples and monasteries that form a half-circle round the walled-in park of the Summer Palace in Jehol would be as boring as a guide-book, and I have limited myself to the two most famous temples, the Potala, which is associated with the return of the Torgot, and Hsin-kung, whose temple halls still retain memories of the third Tashi Lama, and his visit to Jehol and Peking. But it is impossible to ignore two of the stately temple-monasteries situated at the foot of the hills, which are bordered on the east by the Jehol river valley. We drove past them on the way to Hsin-kung. From among the desolate hills rose their magnificent façades and glittering roofs; only the river separated us from them, but we were delayed, for the car stuck fast in the river-bed, and it was not until we had sent for some help from the nearest village that we eventually reached the other side.

A path led up hills and through ravines to the stately Ili-miao temple. Even that short walk took longer than we had anticipated, for, lying among the gravel, wherever one looked, were neolithic tools and implements, such as hammers, axes, and skin-scrapers, and before many minutes had passed we had collected quite a dozen. During his years in Jehol, Father Mullie had made a fine collection. The great Manchu Emperors were not the first who had been charmed with Jehol and had chanted its praises: even so far back as the later stone age, the valleys in the land of the Hachin Mongols were famous for their numerous settlements.

A wall surrounded Ili-miao and its sanctuaries. The Lama who had the keys let us in through the main gate in the south wall, and we stepped into a stone-paved forecourt and stopped before an enormous incense-bowl on a stone pedestal. In front of us rose the imposing façade of the main temple. The lower half was built of stone and bricks, with square windows and three round-arched gateways surrounded by graceful ornamentation. The upper half was of woodwork, in three stories, with a similar number of tiled roofs, each one smaller than the one below. (Pl. XXI.)

When we entered the temple-hall we stood still, amazed at the magnificence of the building, the picturesque columns, and impressed beyond measure by the play of the soft lighting. Steps led up to the first gallery where twilight reigned and the columns glimmered pale against the dusky background. The upper gallery was brightly lighted, for there all the windows were open, the sun shone in, and reflections from the bright summer day played and danced.

To stand on the stone floor below and look up at these lofty spaces was like seeing the colonnades of a dream castle. Everything loomed up in such light, airy, tender tones; the columns were silhouetted against a still lighter background, and the whole seemed to glow with the magic of the Mountain-King's castle. (Pl. XXIII.)

Galleries ran round all four sides of the temple, their sagging floors covered with the dust and litter of seventy years—for that was when they were last swept. The roof was divided into square, beautifully decorated panels, and between the capitals of the columns stretched broad friezes, ornamented with Buddhas in large medallions.

The place of honour in Ili-miao was occupied by a gigantic image of the goddess Târâ, glittering with gold, and rising out of the chalice of a lotus flower. Her dress fell in graceful folds, she wore bracelets and a necklace, and on her head was a five-pointed crown. Behind her rose a mighty gilded aureole of magnificently carved wood, in a pattern of tendrils, leaves and flowers: (Pl. XXII.)

We were told that this sanctuary was P'u-t'u-tien (the Temple of All Preservation). Professor O. Franke calls it An-yüan-miao (the Temple for the Pacifying of the Far Dwellers). In daily speech it is spoken of as Yü-lin-miao (the Temple of the Elm Grove), but we generally heard the simple name Ili-miao. Built in 1764, it was principally intended as a compliment to the Dzungar tribe of twelve hundred men who, in 1759, had settled in that district. It is said to have been modelled after Ku'rh-cha-tu-kang, an old sanctuary on the north bank of the river Ili which in the days of Galdan Tsering was greatly venerated by the Dzungar. The temple on the Ili river was destroyed during the Manchu Emperors' wars, and Ch'ien-lung had a replica built at Jehol to comfort those who had come from so far.

Leaving Ili-miao, and going over hills and ravines towards the south, we came, after a walk of about half a mile, to the strange and original sanctuary which bears the name P'u-lo-tien, the Temple of Universal Delight, or, according to Franke, P'u-lo-szŭ, the Temple of the Penetrating Joy. The date of the building was 1767, and the main hall is dedicated to "Buddha, the King of the Highest Joy". On the memorial tablet the Emperor speaks of the Dzungars joining the kingdom, and says that the princes of that great Mongolian race came yearly to Jehol for an audience. The temple was built so that even in Jehol they could live according to their traditions and their faith. "At which their joy will be great."

We entered a courtyard, where weeds were growing up between the paving-stones ; on all four sides it was surrounded by pavilions whose lines were noble and harmonious. The building on the north, Tsung-yin-tien, contained three big, well-preserved images. (Pls. XXIV and XXVI.) Passing through the round arch of a *p'ai-lou* we came to the lowest of three walled terraces. A double flight of steps, with balustrades, led upwards to the middle terrace, which was surrounded by a delicate fretted marble balustrade, and on which stood eight tall *stupas* of porcelain, coloured bright green and gold. The tops of these reliquaries had been removed, either from pure mischief or because of their beauty and value. (Pl. XXV.)

On the topmost terrace rose the chief temple, P'u-lo-tien, its beautiful lines and shapes reminiscent of the Temple of Heaven in Peking. It was round, and had two roofs. The lower story rested on an outer ring of columns, while the upper portion, shaped like a mushroom, was supported by twelve tall, free-standing columns, in the interior of the hall itself. (Pl. XXVII.)

In front of this was a large round plinth of beautifully ornamented marble, about seven feet high, whose smooth top supported a kind of tabernacle or shrine of brown wood. Inside this, hidden from the eyes of the world, was a God of Copulation with a woman in his arms.

From whatever direction one looked at P'u-lo-tien, it presented a pleasing and attractive appearance. Seen from the desolate hills, it showed up to advantage among the surrounding pavilions. It was just as beautiful when seen from the forecourt where the tall pine-trees grew and where, at the slightest breeze, all the roof-bells tinkled as if the spirits of the air were speaking with their voices.

To the east of this temple, on the top of the highest of the eastern hills, was a natural pillar that was like a ruined tower. This column, visible from the whole of the surrounding country, is caused by erosion, and the Chinese call it, aptly enough, 'The Batlet'.

P'u-shan-szŭ, the Temple of Universal Goodness, and P'u-jên-szŭ, the Temple of Universal Love (Pl. XXVIII), were both built by the Mongol princes in honour of the Emperor K'ang-hsi's sixtieth birthday, 1713; in a memorial tablet in the latter is the famous stanza:

> "Wonderful in all its beauty
> Dreams the Jehol river strand.
> May great spirits ever bless thee,
> Boundary of our fosterland."

When we had re-crossed the river, we went towards Hsin-kung, which competes with the Potala for the honour of being the largest and most magnificent Lama-temple in Jehol.

Of Hsin-kung (the New Palace), to give it its common name (its full name is Hsü-mi-fu-shou-miao, or "The Temple of the Mountainous Good Fortune and Honourable Old Age"), Franke says, rightly, that it is "the most splendid of all Jehol's temples, and one of the most beautiful monuments of antiquity in the kingdom of China." The Chinese name is a flowery translation of the Tibetan *fu-shou*, which, like *Tashi*, means 'luck' and 'long life', and *hsü-mi* is the same word as *Sumeru*, the Sanskrit name of the legendary mountain to the north of India, whose Tibetan name is *Lunpo* (Pl. XXXIX).

The gateways of Hsin-kung were orientated in the

same way as those of the Potala, and, as in that temple, the entrance was through a park of scattered pines and firs ; but the ground sloped less steeply than that of its neighbour.

Before the southern gate we came first to a square stone building which arched above a gigantic tortoise of white marble. With extraordinary power and skill the sculptor had depicted the head and shell of the symbolic animal, its highly conventionalized shape and proportion being quite graceful. On its back the tortoise supported a vertical, oblong pillar of stone, the short sides of which were carved with dragons and tendrils in high relief, while the front and back were engraved with the Emperor Ch'ien-lung's records of the founding of the temple. At each of the cardinal points was a rounded archway, through which blew the four winds of heaven, making it pleasantly cool in the tortoise house during the hottest summer days. (Pl. XXIX.)

The record was composed by the Emperor himself and was another link in the political chain with which he bound the followers of Lamaism to his Dragon Throne.

He speaks of the blossoming of "The Yellow Doctrine" ever since the days of Tsong-kha-pa, the Reformer ; of the divine succession of the Dalai Lama and the Tashi Lama, and of the building of Hsin-kung "as a place for meditation and devotion" for the latter. He says that in this respect he was following the example of his august ancestor,

Shun-chih (1644–61), who built the Yellow Temple in Peking as a dwelling-place for the fifth Dalai Lama. Characteristically, the Emperor declares that the latter came because he was sent for, "while the Tashi Lama approached us in person, not because he was summoned, but because it was his own desire to come to Peking to see how Chinese rule fosters the growth of the Yellow Doctrine, how it promotes the good of mankind, and how in that wide world perfect freedom reigns, and the people and their possessions enjoy an assured peace."

He reminds us once more of his seventieth birthday and the cause for rejoicing now that all the Mongol races are under Chinese rule. He certainly desired no homage on his birthday, but, as the Tashi Lama wished to come, he could not be prevented.

We shall come later to the political game that was going on behind the scenes, and with which was involved the visit of the third Tashi Lama (or, as the Mongols and Chinese call him, Panchen Erdeni Lama) to Jehol and Peking.

Now we continued our wanderings up fifty steps, and through the arched gateways of a *p'ai-lou* of coloured faience, to a stately rectangular stone building, remarkable for its harmonious architecture, which was faintly reminiscent of an Italian Renaissance palace. Like the Potala this was merely a shell of stone and brick built round the holy temple. (Pl. XXXVIII.)

The windows were decorated with artistic lintels

and projecting friezes of green faience which contrasted effectively with the light red tones of the vast walls.

As in the Potala, this huge palace-like stone building surrounded a square courtyard, most of which was taken up by a splendidly decorated pavilion. The unbuilt-on portion of the courtyard was narrower than in the Potala, for in Hsin-kung, all four sides were complete with galleries. We had to be careful when we walked over their swaying floors. The woodwork was frail; ruin and decay were imminent, and it cannot be long before these inner galleries suffer the same fate as those in the Potala, and collapse. We went from one room to another, finding in each innumerable small niches intended for Buddhas, but the niches were empty; the Buddhas had been stolen and scattered like chaff before the wind. In the temples at Jehol only such images remain as are too heavy to drag away. (Pl. XXXIX.)

The roof-terrace of Hsin-kung, with its square stone-flags, was still in a good state of preservation, and from it there was an uninterrupted view in all directions. To the south was the Lion Valley, and, on the other side, hills over which the grey stone wall round the part of the Summer Palace writhed like a serpent of solid stone. To the west-north-west we could see the Potala with its gateways, dormitories, temples, and green pine-trees. To the east-south-east rose the Ili-miao, on the other side of the river, and everywhere we looked was smiling, undulating country.

Beneath us to the south was the colourful, glittering *p'ai-lou* and the house of the tortoise, and, on the roof itself, were small corner shrines which still contained images and altars. Our eyes were caught immediately by the golden double roofs of Hsin-kung's most famous temple pavilion, that standing in the square courtyard, for they were the most richly and artistically decorated of all the roofs in Jehol. Eight scaly, gilded copper dragons, with raised heads, humped backs, and twisting tails, kept watch over the temple and its gods, and, on the lower roof, eight golden sea-elephants lifted their trunks like awe-inspiring Spirits of the Air, with trumpets raised. (Pl. XXX, XLI and XLIV.)

In the sunset the dragons and elephants shone like gold. The pines in the parks glowed fiery red, and the rust-coloured walls took on shades of volcanic intensity in the afterglow. The shadows lengthened and another night crept over Jehol. The gloom that always reigned in Hsin-kung's enclosed temple halls deepened, and it was only with difficulty that we could make out the few gods who still bent their dreaming faces over the altars.

In Hsin-kung, as in the Potala, the Tibetan and Chinese styles of architecture were intermingled in a pleasing and effective manner. The main temples, containing the sanctuaries, were purely Chinese; the great surrounding walls and the dormitories, Tibetan.

I was greatly tempted to pass a night in the starlight

on the roof-terrace of Hsin-kung, listening to the tinkle of the small bells on the corners of the pavilion-roofs. I should have loved to spend a night in the magnificent temple-halls, but my proposal met with no encouragement. Both the authorities and the monks would have suspected dark deeds, and perhaps it would have been an uneasy night, for I might have been kept awake by whispering, creeping foot-steps behind the altars and columns. The golden gods might have opened their eyes, and descended from their seats in the hearts of the lotus flowers to drive out the presumptuous mortal who disturbed their rest, and perhaps our own rest would have been disturbed by the temple rats, lizards, and centipedes.

Chapter V

SOME OTHER TEMPLES IN JEHOL

About half a mile east-north-east of Hsin-kung and a mile north of Ili-miao, at the foot of the hills, stood the temple of Ta-fo-szŭ (the Temple of the Great Buddha). We set out for this temple on the first of July. Its real name is P'u-ning-szŭ (the Temple of Pervading Peace). It was built by Ch'ien-lung in 1755 to commemorate the subjugation of the Dzungars. Franke reproduces the inscription on the memorial tablet which relates how, in the autumn of 1755, the princes and noblemen of the four *oirad*, or tribes of the Choros, Durbet, Khoit and Khoshoit, assembled in Jehol to do homage to the Emperor. At a festal banquet in the Palace was celebrated the union of the " eight inner Banners and forty-nine outer Banners, the four Khalkha tribes, and the newly joined Dzungars, who, together with the peoples of the interior, will henceforth form one big family."

At the gatehouse in the south wall stood a lonely guardian tree, a leafy, shade-giving acacia. At last we reached a square courtyard, shut in as usual by four pavilions in Chinese temple style. The finest of these, which faced south, was oblong, and, upon

XXIX. The tortoise supporting the record tablet in Hsin-kung (p. 75)

XXX. The temple pavilion of Hsin-kung (p. 78)

XXXI. The principal pavilion at the Yellow Temple at Peking (p. 111)

XXXII. *Stupa* erected in the park of the Yellow Temple in memory of the third Tashi Lama (p. 111)

XXXIII. The Emperor K'ang Hsi in his prime

XXXIV. The Emperor K'ang Hsi in old age

XXXV. The Copper Temple in the park of the Summer Palace (p. 130)

XXXVI. The Emperor Ch'ien Lung in middle age (p. 199)

the long wall directly opposite the entrance, sat three gilded Buddhas, about sixteen feet high. They were alike except for the positions of the hands, which signified the various symbolic functions. In front of them were an altar-table with offering-bowls and the usual ceremonial objects of the Lama cult. On both the short sides, to east and west, were the Eighteen Lohans (Buddha's disciples), nine on each side. (Pl. XLVIII.) These were made of wood, while the ritual objects were of wood or bronze, rather roughly made. A big temple-bell of iron hung in one frame, and in another was a flat drum.

The hall of the gods in Ta-fo-szŭ differed from all the others we had seen in that it was excellently preserved and seemed well cared for. The roof was beautifully painted in the most decorative patterns. A lama stepped forward, bowed, and lighted sticks of incense in a bronze bowl half full of ashes.

Forty-one steps led up to another courtyard surrounded by temples, pavilions, and pagodas in both Chinese and Tibetan style, some surrounded by balustrades of fretted white marble in lovely patterns, each vertical post being surmounted by a tall knob. (Pl. XLIX.)

From that courtyard we could not glance in any direction without seeing the most beautiful and satisfying architectural perspectives, the most imposing being the main temple, Ta-fo-szŭ, a massive building of reddish-brown wood with five roofs, and free-standing columns, the whole resting on a stone terrace four feet high, to which three flights of steps with marble balustrades led from the courtyard below. The centre flight was divided by an inclined stone slope of white marble with an artistically carved dragon in high relief.

The five roofs, rising one above the other, diminished in size towards the top, and from the turned-up corners hung bells that rang out in honour of the Spirits of the Air. (Pl. LXI.)

We entered the temple. Two galleries ran all round it. Though it was by no means small, it was filled by the gigantic group of gods who had their home there. In the middle, towering up as far as the topmost roof, was the great Buddha, said to be over seventy-two feet high. It was of wood, glittering with gold and colours. On either side stood slightly smaller figures. (Pl. L.)

When we went up two stories and reached the first gallery, we were only on a level with the navel of the gigantic Buddha, and his head, sharply foreshortened, disappeared in the higher regions. Even from the upper gallery it was impossible to get a full view of the figure. It was too big in proportion to the hall, and we could never get far enough away to see it properly. From the stone floor we could study the pedestal and the vast feet; from the first gallery the stomach; and, from the upper one, the shoulders, arms, and head.

We did not do anything more that day, as there were important functions that could not be neglected.

General Tang Yü-lin had invited us to a banquet in his *yamen*, formerly the dwelling-place of the last Emperor of the dynasty. A messenger came from the *yamen* to fetch our visiting-cards and informed us that it was time to start.

At the great gateway, sentries presented arms, and a tall colonel who was acting as adjutant or chamberlain, received us and led us to a pavilion where musicians played as we entered. The General greeted us and made us welcome, and we were presented to several important officials who were our fellow-guests. We were surrounded by a crowd of servants, officers, and soldiers.

We were invited to sit down at an oblong table and tea and cigarettes were handed round. Then Father Mullie, three officials, and our party were taken to the General's table, while the other guests took their places at another table. The dinner was excellent. We were offered the finest Chinese delicacies—a swallow's-nest soup, a tree fungus from Szechuan, sharks' fins, bamboo shoots, lotus buds, chicken, fish, pork, with delicious crisp crackling, and finally rice, which is invariably the sign that a meal is finished. We drank cognac and beer and were not obliged to drink more than we wished. All the time, musicians were playing in the park, occasionally European tunes, but mostly military marches.

The next day, after the Minister for Education, Chang I-ting, had paid us a visit in order to see my sketches, we drove with Father Mullie to the " Temple of the Five Hundred Buddhas ", Lo-han-t'ang, or the " Hall of Buddha's Lohans " (or disciples), which was situated to the west-north-west of the Potala, on the north slope of the Lion Valley. It was built in 1774. In the great temple we walked through a perfect labyrinth of aisles between double rows of the five hundred Lohans, carved in wood, gilded, and of life size. Many of them wore thin yellow mantles, the gifts of pious believers. One could walk and walk through those long aisles and gaze with delight at those countless silent saints, sitting there meditating in every imaginable attitude ; some with outstretched hands, others with hands raised upwards, or with one hand resting on a knee while the other touched the forehead, and others held their hands as if they were expounding the holy writings to a gathering of disciples. Some looked serious and meditative, others smiling and ironic, and there were some carved with such inimitable humour that they would have done excellently as caricatures in a comic paper. (Pls. LII–LV.)

The temple had a drum-tower and a clock-tower. Like everything else in Jehol, even that sanctuary was falling in ruin. In one corner, the roof had fallen in ; beams and planks hung by a thread, so that it was dangerous to pass underneath them. The sunlight streamed through the gaping holes, and that part of the temple was at least well lighted. Many of the Lohans had been moved so that they might not be utterly ruined by rain and snow.

Between Lo-han-t'ang and the Potala there was yet another temple, Shu Hsiang-szŭ, which was striking by reason of the excellent state of preservation of the hall (Pl. LVI), with its three tall Buddhas, and, in front of them, an almost naked, jovially grinning figure with swollen belly and puffy fingers. This was lighted by the daylight which poured through the open doors, and the shining gold conjured up an effect of greasy well-being. His head was bald, his eyes almost shut, and his ears so long that the lobes rested on his shoulders, symbolizing his ability to hear and know everything. A scanty mantle was draped over his arms and legs, but it was far too small to hide his swelling paunch. The throne upon which he sat with up-drawn knees was very plain and solid, and matched the substantial body.

If one were to make an exhaustive examination of such images of the gods as still remain in Jehol, and write an explanation of each one, the result would be a very valuable treatise on Buddhist-Lamaist iconography, but it is evident that such a task is outside the scope of the present work. Still, in order to give a slight idea of what such a work would be, I will include the following information given to me by Professor Lessing concerning the "Laughing Buddha".

He tells me that this strange personality, half god and half saint, may very possibly have had its origin in a group of short-legged, pot-bellied images of gods, who, in India, played the part of door and wealth gods.

It is a recognized fact that Buddhist art in India was largely influenced by the art of the late classic age in Greece and Further Asia, and if, in accordance with this fact, we look for a prototype of the Laughing Buddha, we must go back to Silenus, not the classic Silenus, but a more popular one, who was represented with short legs, fat belly, and bald head, and provided with a wine-skin ; one who, in his character as a friend of youth, was generally surrounded by playing children. Silenus was the tutor of the boy Bacchus. If this assumption is correct, Professor Lessing notes the following similarities between the god in question and the Silenus types—short legs, pot belly, bald head, a smile which, in the Chinese representations, is changed into a broad grin more in keeping with the grotesque body. An inadequate mantle has taken the place of the wine-skin, and the children are used to interpret the six senses (i.e. the five senses and *manas*, the " sensorium commune " of our schoolmen). Often the children are eighteen in number, signifying that they then represent the transcendent bearers of the six powers of perception, that is, the six senses themselves, and the six seats of the senses, all of which are represented by children. Professor Lessing points out that we can also conceive of the naked representation of the Nile God as a prototype of the Buddhist saint in question. The Nile God too was surrounded by children, their number signifying the number of feet the Nile rose.

As far as we know, the spiritual importance of the

Pot-bellied Buddha is purely Chinese, even if somewhat intermingled with outside influences. In the official Book of Legends he is called Ch'i-tzŭ, or Pu-tai-ho-shang, the " Bonze with the Hemp Sack ", because he carried a sack into which he put everything he could beg. Possibly this was developed from the wine-skin of Silenus. Pu-tai means " food-sack ", a play on words regarding his corpulent person. Finally he also goes under the name Ta-tu-tzŭ (Mi-lo) fo, the Pot-bellied (Maitreya) Buddha, which seems to have had its origin in the last, falsely interpreted, words that, according to the legend, he is supposed to have uttered before his death.

Legend places him in the T'ang, or the later Liang, dynasty, between the seventh and tenth centuries A.D. He is described as having been very fat and of a gloomy countenance ; the latter characteristic being quite opposed to all his more recent representations. Sometimes he was silent, at others talkative, and, on a staff resting across his shoulder, he carried a sack in which he put everything he came across, and this gave rise to one of his names. He could sleep wherever he happened to be, undisturbed by the weather. Once when he was discovered sleeping in a snowstorm people observed that no snow had fallen on his body. At another time he was seen standing for a long time on a bridge, as if he were looking for something. " O worthy one, what do you seek ? " he was asked. " Mankind ! " was his laconic answer. His prophecies always came true. If it were fine weather and he was seen wearing thick-soled sandals, people knew that there would be rain ; and if it were raining and he wore straw sandals they knew that it would soon be fine again. He lived a wandering life, which he celebrated in the following verses :

> " A begging bowl holds rice from a thousand houses,
> Alone I wander my thousand miles.
> In the early morning I see few people,
> Then I ask my way of the white clouds."

Once—legend places the date as 916 A.D.—he was found sitting under an overhanging rock. He said :

> " Mi-lo (Maitreya), O truthful Mi-lo
> Countless times re-born,
> Time after time manifesting yourself to men of to-day,
> Yet the men of to-day have never comprehended you." [1]

With these words he entered into Nirvāna.

According to another legend, his death occurred in the period T'ien-fu (901–4). The inhabitants of the district in which he died are said to have buried him, but afterwards he was to be seen elsewhere with his sack on his back.

We left the Buddha with the pot belly to his lonely dreams, and went up a flight of steps to an open pavilion which consisted of a mushroom-shaped roof resting on columns. It was set up on a stone terrace surrounded by a parapet. On a magnificent marble

[1] In these farewell words people thought they read his intention of referring to himself as Maitreya. His reputation grew as time passed, and he came more and more to be looked upon as a forerunner of the Buddhist Messiah. For that reason it became customary to put his image in the entrance halls of temples.—(Lessing.)

XXXVII. One of the Four Guardians of the Copper Temple (p. 130)

XXXVIII. The Temple and Monastery buildings of Hsin-kung (p. 76)

XXXIX. The Temple courtyard of Hsin-kung (p. 77)

XI. Bronze statue of the third Tashi Lama (p. 100)

XLI. The roof of the Golden Pavilion at Hsin-kung (p. 78)

XLII. Detail of the Tashi Lama's monument at the Yellow Temple

XLIII. The west pavilion at Hsin-kung

XLIV. Hsin-kung (p. 78)

socle, decorated with finely carved dragon and flower ornamentation, and directly under the pavilion roof, was a divinity riding on a terrible monster that resembled a lion. On either side of him were bodyguards or custodians. Folk-lore says that the rider on the lion is a divine representation of the Emperor Ch'ien-lung. (Pls. LVII and LVIII.)

Between this temple and Lo-han-t'ang lay the ruins of an old farm. Here is the tale that Father Mullie told us concerning it. Once the Emperor Yung-chêng went to the apartments of his Empress to drink tea. Among the slave girls who were serving them he noticed one who had a very sweet face but whose head was disfigured by two patches of white. To tease the Empress he said that the young girl's appearance attracted him, and the Empress, annoyed, replied that if she pleased him he had better take her away. He did so. After a time she became pregnant, but as she was not a recognized concubine, she feared that she would be put to death. When her time drew near she was with the Empress's court at Jehol. The gates in the park wall were carefully watched, and no one might go in or out without stating his errand. In her despair, the young girl fled to that part of the wall where the tall pagoda now stands, and the wall opened to let her through, afterwards closing behind her. She hurried through the Lion Valley but could get no farther than the farm between the two temples, of which only the ruins now remain. She found sanctuary with the farmer's family, and there a boy was born. When the Emperor heard what had happened to the young girl, his heart was touched and he publicly recognized the child as his son. In the fullness of time that son became the great Emperor Ch'ien-lung. Alas, the story is not true, for Ch'ienlung was born in Peking.

We often had to go to the Potala on business, for our wonderfully clever architect, Mr. W. H. Liang, was working there. He had been recommended to us by Mr. Anner in Peking. It was Mr. Liang who, after much negotiation, had undertaken to produce an absolutely faithful replica of the most renowned temple pavilion in the Potala. Even before our visit to Jehol, I had realized that this building was the most beautiful and decorative that could be found in China or Mongolia, and that no other would be so well fitted to adorn one of the large parks in Chicago. It would indeed be an admirable gift to the city from my countryman, Mr. Vincent Bendix. To be sure I had only seen photographs of it, taken in December by Dr. Montell upon his first visit to Jehol. The original was far more wonderful than the photographs. There, fresh but subdued, were the original Chinese mineral colours in all their splendour, and it was not difficult to visualize how beautiful that red temple with its gilded copper roofs would look surrounded by leafy, green trees.

Mr. Liang was busily employed in making plans and specifications, and taking measurements of the columns, beams, carved planks, windows, capitals, and friezes. Not the smallest detail in the whole of that complicated building escaped his eye; he had everything so clear in his notes and sketches and in his head that whenever and wherever he desired he could set up an absolutely faithful replica of the original.

He had brought from Peking a very clever master-painter, an elderly man who refurnished the temple rooms to fit into Mr. Liang's design. He moved an altar-table to the open door in order to have a good light, improvised a bench, spread out his paper, pencils, rulers, dividers, brushes and colours, and there he sat all day until sunset, copying the patterns on the carved and painted beams and capitals. He was always friendly and jovial, and peered waggishly from behind his big spectacles when one went to look at his fine, cleverly executed sketches. Occasionally he would take a pull at his pipe but, apart from that, he worked unceasingly and put all his heart and soul into his copying.

Later, in Peking, we signed a contract with Mr. Liang. All those parts of the temple that could be made in China were to be ready for shipment by the spring of 1931; the rest, such as the stone terraces, brick walls, columns and rougher beams could be made just as well, if not better, in Chicago, and, above all, they would be cheaper, as the expenses of transport would be avoided.

Only after the temple had been erected under the direction of Dr. Montell in its park in Chicago could the final painting be done, under the supervision of

Mr. Liang, by five Chinese craftsmen, three painters and two carpenters, with the help of workmen from Chicago. Mr. Liang was extremely pleased that no American colours were to be used, only real Chinese ones that never fade or lose their subdued, discreet tones, and last a hundred years. The most careful calculations had to be made of the amount of each colour that would be required, and these were to be prepared and ground in Peking, so that only the final mixing with oil would be required when the painting was to be done.

Just before we finally left Jehol we paid farewell visits to the governor, General Tang Yü-lin, two other officials, the New Zealand missionary, Mr. Duthy and his wife, and the son of the governor. The latter took us to a house where, under proper protection, a dozen very fine bronzes were preserved. They are said to date from the Chou era, but possibly are not so old.

Not far from there we saw the Temple of Confucius, in the hall of the main pavilion of which there are several memorial tablets and other objects (Pl. LIX). In a smaller kiosk the records were supported by a stone tortoise like that in Hsin-kung, but smaller. The Emperor Ch'ien-lung is said to have founded the Temple of Confucius. It was surrounded by a small park, and the pine trees planted round the main hall formed a kind of outer cloister which accorded perfectly with the beautifully made columns.

At the top of several flights of steps we came to a

higher pavilion, raised to commemorate the father and grandfather of Confucius, and enclosing their ancestral tablets. The whole building was very well preserved, but even here there were weeds and bushes growing out of the roofs, and ruin was imminent.

CHAPTER VI

THE VISIT OF THE TASHI LAMA TO JEHOL [1]

IN the records on the stone supported by the tortoise at the entrance to Hsin-kung, the Emperor Ch'ien-lung gives as one of the reasons for the building of that stately sanctuary the coming of the third Tashi Lama to the Summer Palace.

By building a special monastery-temple and giving it the same name—Tashi-lhunpo—as the Tashi Lama's own monastery in Tibet, the Emperor showed the Prince of the Church in Tibet the greatest courtesy, while, at the same time, he explained that he was only following the example set by his august ancestor, the Emperor Shun-chih, when he built the Yellow Temple in Peking as a sanctuary for the fifth Dalai Lama.

With this visit were associated the following events :

[1] Sources used for the following chapter :

Rockhill, W. W. : *The Dalai Lamas of Lhasa and their relations with the Manchu Emperors of China*, 1644–1908 (Leyden, 1910).

Markham : *Narrative of the Mission of George Bogle to Tibet* (London, 1879), pp. 83 *sqq.*

Turner, Samuel : *Account of an Embassy to the Court of the Teshoo Lama in Tibet* (London, 1800).

Amiot : *Mémoires concernant l'histoire, etc., des chinois*, Vol. IX, (Paris, 1783), pp. 446 *sqq.*

In 1616, the year in which the Torgot fled to Russia, the fifth Dalai Lama was re-incarnated in his successor Lobsang Gyatzo (bLo-bsang Gya-mtsho), who, at the age of six, took up his residence in the monastery of Debung, near Lhasa.

At that time the three provinces of Tibet, Wu (U or Wei), with its capital, Lhasa; Tsang, with its capital, Tashi-lhunpo, and Kham, were ruled by the royal dynasty—P'agmo-du.

After many religious disputes between the sects of the red and yellow lamas, in about the year 1630 supreme power over the whole country was seized by P'unts'og Nam-gyal. This meant that the very existence of the yellow sect was threatened, and the Dalai Lama, who was the head of the yellow sect, and an earthly incarnation of Avalokiteśvara, called upon the Eleut Mongols in Koko-nor for help. Their chief, Gushi Khan, himself belonged to the yellow sect. In 1638, the province of Kham came under his rule and that of the yellow sect. Together with his kinsmen, the northern Eleuts and the Torgot, Gushi Khan obeyed the summons of the Prince of the Church. In 1641 he conquered the whole of Tibet and for a time was its ruler under the Dalai Lama, but he soon surrendered all power, except the command of the Mongolian army of occupation, to the latter. At the same time the Grand Lama removed his residence to Lhasa, where, on a hill, he built the famous Potala Monastery. Even before that the Dalai and Tashi Lamas had sent an important Hutuktu (Living

Buddha) to the Emperor in Mukden. The envoy bore letters and presents. When the 'living Buddha' returned he brought a letter from the Emperor to the Dalai Lama, Gushi Khan, and the other potentates.

This was the foundation of the alliance between Tibet and Ta-ch'ing (the Manchu dynasty).

In 1648 the Chinese government sent Hsi-la-pu Gelong to the Dalai and Tashi Lamas with gifts, and an invitation to come and visit the Emperor in Peking. The Dalai Lama accepted, but the Tashi Lama excused himself on account of his great age.

The Dalai Lama set out, and, in the middle of 1652, with his following of three thousand men, he had reached Ordos. From there he sent a letter to the Emperor asking him to come in person and meet him in Kuei-hua-chêng, or some other place. Astounded at such a request, the Emperor summoned the princes to a council. The Manchus advised him to go, because by so doing he could win the trust of the Khalkha Mongols ; the Chinese advised the Emperor, " who is the world's greatest monarch and ruler ", not to go and meet the Grand Lama, and not even to allow him to come within the Chinese borders, but to send a prince to him with gifts.

The Emperor's greatest fear was that, if he refused the Grand Lama's request, the latter would turn back to Tibet, and the Khalkha Mongols would not acknowledge Chinese suzerainty. In the end he made the excuse that he could not leave, as he had to be in constant communication with his troops who were

XLV. The Tomb of Hsiang Fei (p. 215)

XLVI. Hsiang Fei in armour (p. 222)

XLVII. Ho Shên, the favourite of Ch'ien Lung (p. 236)

XLVIII. Ta-fo-szŭ: two of the eighteen Lohans (p. 81)

XLIX. The main courtyard at Ta-fo-szŭ (p. 81)

L. The Great Buddha (p. 82)

LI. View across the valley from Ta-fo-szŭ

LII. Lo-han-t'ang: the courtyard (p. 84)

operating in the south-west part of his kingdom. Instead he would send princes and mandarins of the first rank to meet the Grand Lama, and he himself would receive him at the borders of his kingdom.

After further negotiations, the Dalai Lama decided to continue his journey to Peking, where he was received in the Yellow Temple, situated outside the north wall of the town. In that same temple, the present Dalai Lama stayed, when he came to Peking in 1908.

At the end of 1652 the Dalai Lama was given his first audience, overwhelmed with gifts, and honoured by banquets; but after only a month, he bade the Emperor farewell, making the excuse that the climate did not suit him or his suite. Upon his departure he was given ceremonial gifts consisting of horses, gold, silver, pearls, jades and silk, and an illustrious title engraved on a plaque of gold.

The Grand Lama returned through the Nank'ou Pass, over Kalgan and the Lamaist lands. The Emperor realized, as did his successors after him, that if the dynasty wished to keep the Mongols under their suzerainty, the Dalai Lama was their most powerful ally.

Since that meeting one hundred and thirty years had passed, and now, once again, a Prince of the Church of equally high rank was coming to the capital of the kingdom and the Summer Palace in Jehol.

In the Emperor Ch'ien-lung's own records in Hsin-kung, we cannot fail to notice the eagerness with which he emphasises the fact that—unlike the Dalai Lama one hundred and thirty years before—the Tashi Lama was coming on his own initiative and by his own wish. The Emperor had not the slightest desire to trouble him, any more than anyone else, to bring his good wishes for his birthday, but, when the Tashi Lama himself had asked for an audience, it would have been unbecoming to refuse him or prevent his journey. And now when the Grand Lama arrived, he would find in Jehol a temple-monastery, a copy of the Tashi-lhunpo, where he would feel at home, and could give himself up to meditation.

But, if we compare the Emperor's statement with contemporary English accounts of the reasons for the Tashi Lama's visit, we get a very different conception of the whole affair.

At that time the great Warren Hastings, in the service of the East India Company, was the first Governor-General of India. In 1774 a boundary war had broken out between the English and the Rajah of Bhutan. The Tashi Lama wrote to Warren Hastings begging him to cease hostilities. The wise Governor-General decided to take this opportunity to investigate the political situation and commercial possibilities of Tibet, its geography and natural products, and see whether there was any possibility of opening trade relations with that snowy land in the north. He sent Mr. George Bogle with letters and presents to the Grand Lama. Bogle was well received and stayed the whole winter of 1774–5 in Tashilhunpo.

In audience, the Grand Lama sat on his throne of gold, wearing a yellow monk's robe, with a tall yellow mitre on his head. The envoy delivered the Governor-General's letters and presents and was given a *khadak* (a scarf made of thin silk nearly seven feet long) by the Tashi Lama.

On later occasions Bogle was received without ceremony :

> " . . . after two or three visits the Lama used (except on holidays) to receive me without any ceremony, his head uncovered, dressed only in the large red petticoat which is worn by all the *gylongs*, red Bulgar boots, a yellow cloth vest with his arms bare and a piece of coarse yellow cloth thrown across his shoulders. He sat sometimes in a chair, sometimes on a bench covered with tiger-skins, and nobody but the *Sopon Chumbo* present. Sometimes he would walk with me about the room and explain to me the pictures, and make remarks upon the colour of my eyes, etc." [1]

Bogle gives a very sympathetic description of the third Tashi Lama :

> " The Teshu Lama is about 40 years of age, and of low stature and, though not corpulent, rather inclined to be fat. His complexion is fairer than that of most of the Tibetans, and his arms are as white as those of a European ; his hair, which is jet black, is cut very short, his beard and whiskers never above a month long . . . I endeavoured to find out in his character those defects which are inseparable from humanity, but he is so universally beloved that I had no

[1] *Narrative of the Mission of George Bogle to Tibet*, Clements R. Markham, C.B., F.R.S. (London, 1876), p. 84.

success, and not a man could find it in his heart to speak ill of him." (Pl. XL.)[1]

All the people of Eastern Asia honoured him, for he was omnipotent and possessed of divine accomplishments; he was more loved than feared, open, honourable and generous. In conversation he was gay and merry. He treated pilgrims from India with great generosity in return for information concerning Buddha's own country, so that they should talk well of him and spread his renown in far lands. In his conversation with Bogle, the Grand Lama began by asking about the Governor-General's health; then he went on to the peculiarities of different religions, and to the trade-relations between Bengal and Tibet.

Even the question of high politics was touched on. With delicacy and cunning the English emissary sought to lessen the Grand Lama's admiration for the Emperor and his incredible power, and to direct his attention to the benefits offered by the East India Company, but in that game of chess between Warren Hastings and Ch'ien-lung for the friendship of the Grand Lama, the Emperor won, and the victory cost the Tashi Lama his life.

The Tashi Lama spoke openly of his fears of an outbreak of war between China and Russia, because the Emperor was annoyed with the Russians who had offered a sanctuary to the fleeing Torgot. In such an event, he wished to act as an apostle of peace, and

[1] *Narrative of the Mission of George Bogle to Tibet*, Clements R. Markham, C.B., F.R.S. (London, 1876), p. 84.

hoped that he would be able to count on the support of the East India Company. In the event of Warren Hastings sending embassies to Tibet later on, he should send Hindoos, not Englishmen, for the *Ambans* in Lhasa would not tolerate Europeans within the borders of the Snow Land.

The *Ambans* were two high officials, who represented the power of the Emperor in Lhasa. They reported everything to Peking, and, without doubt, Ch'ien-lung was afraid that with the help of Hastings, the Tashi Lama intended to try and make an end of China's domination in Tibet. So he invited the Grand Lama to Peking, where he hoped to turn his thought into a different channel by the display of an almost magic splendour.

During the years 1777–9, the Emperor sent one invitation after another to the Tashi Lama begging him to visit Peking. The latter excused himself, pleading his fear of small-pox and the dangers of the climate. But the Emperor was insistent.

> " . . . 'My age', says the Emperor, 'is now upwards of seventy years, and the only blessing I can enjoy before I quit this life will be to see you and join in acts of devotion with the divine Teshoo Lama.' The Emperor informed him that houses were erected for the reception of the Lama and his followers upon different places on the road by which he would pass, which had cost upwards of 20 lacks of rupees; that all the inhabitants of that part of China through which his journey lay had orders to have tents, etc., in readiness at all different stages, and that horses, carriages, mules, money, and provisions for the whole retinue, should be in constant readiness at all places and times during the journey.

> The Emperor sent with his letter 1 string of very valuable pearls, 100 pieces of curious silk, by the hands of Leambaw, a trusty person whom he sent to attend the Lama on his journey." [1]

The Emperor even sent letters to the Dalai Lama and other high officials, urging them to persuade the Tashi Lama to come. At last further resistance was in vain. The Supreme Pontiff had to go. To those nearest his person, he confided his suspicions that he would never return.

On the 15th July 1779, he left Tashi-lhunpo, accompanied by a large suite of high dignitaries and monks, and an escort of fifteen hundred men. With him he took valuable presents for the Emperor.

In his following there was a *gosein* or Brahmin priest named Porungheer, whom Warren Hastings had often made use of as a go-between, interpreter, and spy, in Tibet and Bhutan. This man left a very valuable account of the journey of the Tashi Lama, which is to be found in Captain Turner's book. The following is based upon Porungheer's account:

The Tashi Lama travelled on the usual pilgrim's road towards the north-east and, as there is no mention of Lhasa, it looks as if he, like his successor of to-day, had no intercourse with that town. After forty-six days he was met by emissaries of the Emperor, bringing costly gifts and a splendid palan-

[1] *Account of an Embassy to the Court of the Teshoo Lama in Tibet*, Captain Samuel Turner (London, 1800), Appendix 4. *Narrative of the Particulars of the Journey of the Teshoo Lama and his Suite from Tibet to China*, from the verbal report of Porungheer Gosein, pp. 457–8.

quin. At his camp the Lama sat on a platform, and the poor nomads were allowed to touch his feet with their foreheads. After another twenty-one days he was met by eight dignitaries with 2,000 soldiers and, after another nineteen days, he reached the monastery of Kunbum, the birthplace of Tsong-kha-pa, the Reformer, the first incarnation of Amitābha, who was now re-incarnated in the body of the Tashi Lama. A couple of days later winter set in with a heavy fall of snow, and the Grand Lama decided to remain in the monastery. He stayed there four months, and then he received a new letter of welcome from the Emperor, together with five pearl necklaces, a watch, a snuff-box, and a knife, all encrusted with precious stones. The Governor-General of Lanchow arrived, at the order of the Emperor, with 10,000 soldiers and gifts of incredible value.

People surged in thousands to his throne in Kunbum, as they had during his journey. He was constantly importuned by all ranks of people for *a mark of his hand* which, being coloured with *saffron*, he extended, and made a full print of it on a clean piece of paper. Many thousands of these were printed off in the like manner for the multitude that daily surrounded him, which they carefully preserved as the most sacred relics.[1]

One chief gave him 300 horses, 70 mules, 100 camels, 1,000 breadths of brocade, and 40,000 ounces of silver (80,000 silver rupees).

[1] Op. cit., p. 459.

As soon as the spring weather permitted, the Tashi Lama continued his journey, accompanied by the Governor-General of Lanchow and 10,000 soldiers, who, however, left after a week.

In the province of Alashan he was met by the Emperor's son-in-law, who presented him with 100 horses, 100 camels, 20 mules, and 20,000 ounces of silver. The next day nine chiefs came to pay their respects, and presented him with 45,000 ounces of silver, 200 horses, 20 camels, and 500 yaks ; and then they retired.

After twelve days he reached a town where another messenger from the Emperor delivered still another letter of good wishes, a richly decorated two-wheeled cart, drawn by four horses and four mules, a palanquin, real pearls, 200 parcels of yellow silk, flags, etc.

They had travelled for another week towards the capital when the Emperor's eldest son, with the Chief Lama, or grand almoner Chang-chia Hutuktu, came to meet the Holy One, escorted by 10,000 soldiers. More piles of gems, brocades, silks, and ounces of silver were rained on the Tashi Lama, who set off the next day, accompanied by the Prince and the Hutuktu. They had nineteen days' journey to Dolon-nor, where the latter acted as host and presented 40,000 ounces of silver.

After fifteen days the Emperor's younger son and a great following appeared with new gifts, and informed the Grand Lama that it was only a day's journey to the Emperor's Summer Palace in Jehol.

Now the third Tashi Lama made his solemn entry into the Hsin-kung monastery. The next day the Emperor received his guest. A double row of soldiers lined the way between Hsin-kung and the Summer Palace. The Tashi Lama was attended by the Imperial Princes and Mandarins.

> " . . . Upon the Lama etc., entering the inner garden where the Emperor's own Palace is situated the Emperor met him, at a distance of at least forty paces from his throne, on which he usually sat ; and immediately stretching forth his hand, and taking hold of the Lama's, led him towards the throne where, after many salutations and expressions of affection and pleasure on both sides, the Lama was seated by the Emperor upon the uppermost cushion with himself, and at his right hand." [1]

The first conversation only dealt with the honourable guest's health and his long journey, while all the time priceless gifts were being placed on the mats.

It is no exaggeration to say that those two, the worldly prince and the spiritual prince, who at that moment sat together on the Dragon Throne, were the two mightiest men of their time.

The following day the Emperor paid a return visit to Hsin-kung, and asked His Holiness to initiate him into the mysteries of Lamaism :

> " . . . after some indifferent conversation the Emperor then communicated his wishes more at large, with respect to the desire he felt of being instructed in some mysteries of the Lama's religion. They accordingly withdrew, accompanied only by Cheengeea Gooroo (Chang-Chia Hutuktu) to an-

[1] Op. cit., p. 462.

other part of the palace, where three seats were prepared, the one in the centre larger than either of the others in extent, and rising considerably higher, upon which the Lama seated himself, placing the Emperor in that lower, which stood to the right and Cheengeea Gooroo on that at the left. The Lama then, bending his head towards the Emperor, whispered in his ear for about one quarter of an hour, and then setting himself upright, began to whisper aloud certain tenets, or sacred religious sentences, distinctly, which the Emperor and Cheengeea Gooroo continued to repeat after him; and in this manner each sentence was repeated until the Emperor and his Gooroo were perfect in them. This ceremony lasted upwards of three hours whilst their attendants were kept at a considerable distance, in the outer apartments, except two or three devout men whose attendance on the Lama at certain intervals of the ceremony was necessary and were occasionally called in."[1]

For twenty-six days the Tashi Lama remained in Jehol and, at a later meeting, he broached the delicate question of India. He spoke of his splendid friend, Warren Hastings, calling him a prince and regent, and hoped that friendly relations would be established between him and the Emperor.

Very affably, the Emperor promised to comply with such an inexpensive wish, and put several questions about Warren Hastings, India, its size and fighting power, all of which were answered by Porungheer.

After some time the Emperor left Jehol, to make a pilgrimage to the graves of his ancestors. Accompanied by a fitting suite, the Tashi Lama set off for Peking, and, after seven days, reached Huang-szŭ, the Yellow Temple, which had been placed at his disposal.

[1] Op. cit., pp. 462–3.

From Chinese sources we get another version of the manner in which the Emperor received the Tashi Lama:

"The Emperor left Peking . . . the 11th day of the 7th moon (August 10th, 1780), the Panchen Lama arrived from Further Tibet and, kneeling, paid his respects to the Emperor in Tan-p'u-ching.[1]

"The Emperor went to I-ch'ing-k'uang-tien, where he regaled Panchen Lama with tea and fruit. The Lama was granted the favour of sitting. The Emperor ordered him to take up residence in Tashi-lhunpo (Hsin-kung temple). The 14th day (August 13th) the Emperor gave a banquet for Panchen Lama, the princes and others. The 15th day the princes of the Durbet and others came to bring their greetings to the Emperor on his birthday. The Emperor received them in Ch'üan-a-shêng-ching, where he also summoned to the audience the Panchen Lama, the princes and high officials and others, and invited them to partake of tea and fruit. The 3rd day of the 8th moon (1st September) the Emperor received Panchen Lama and the others in Ch'üan-a-shêng-ching for tea. This was repeated on the two following days. On the 11th day he went to the gate of the Summer Palace and there received birthday congratulations from the princes of the Torgot Khans, and the chief of the Korean embassy. The next day the Emperor went to Ch'üan-a-shêng-ching and received for tea the Panchen Lama, princes, high officials, the chief of the Korean embassy and others. The 13th day (September 11th), which was his Majesty's birthday, the Emperor received congratulations from princes, mandarins and others. (The Panchen Lama is not mentioned among those present.) . . . The next day the Emperor entertained them all to tea in the

[1] Mr. T. K. Koo, who translated these records, tells me that the Tashi Lama, according to the Shêng-wu-chi (the account of the Imperial military enterprises), also ko'towed before the Emperor, because the Lama himself insisted upon doing so, although the Emperor only wished him to make the usual obeisance.

same place (The Panchen Lama is not mentioned here either). In the evening the Emperor went to the Garden of Ten Thousand Trees, and gave the Panchen Lama, the princes and others a firework display. This was repeated on the two following days. The 19th day (17th September) the Emperor gave a banquet for the Panchen Lama, princes and others. The 28th day, the Emperor left Jehol and went to the graves of his ancestors. The 2nd day of the 9th moon (29th September) the Emperor arrived at Ku-pei-k'ou, and the 20th day (17th October) he returned to Yüan-ming-yüan (the palace in Peking.)"

In the Palace copy of Ch'i-chü-chu (a diary written by an official of the Han Lin Academy) Mr. Koo found two more accounts of the Emperor's reception of the Tashi Lama—both equally dry and scanty.

"After tea the Emperor went to the three Buddhist temple-halls to burn incense, and the Panchen Lama assisted in the ceremony."

During August and September the Emperor visited Tashi-lhunpo (Hsin-kung) three times to burn incense, but here we are not told whether the Grand Lama assisted at the ceremony or not.

"The 26th day of the 9th moon (23rd October) the Emperor went to Yung-ho-kung (the Imperial Lama-monastery in Peking) and Hsi-Huang-szŭ (the Yellow Temple) to burn incense. The 3rd day of the 10th moon (30th October) the Emperor received the Panchen Lama and Chang-chia Hutuktu at a banquet in Pao-ho-tien ; there were presents of brocade etc." [1]

[1] Mr. Koo tells me that it is scarcely credible that the Emperor allowed the Lama to sit in such an eminent position by his side. An Emperor was bound by certain rules and might not show any one such a courtesy. He could bestow titles and gifts, but not degrade himself. In Tashi-lhunpo there was an Imperial room, where he went when he visited the temple.

In the Chinese archives there is no mention of Ch'ien-lung's visit to the Panchen Lama during the latter's illness; not even of the Grand Lama's death have these records anything to say. In one Chinese account Mr. Koo found a story concerning a monk from "The Western Hills" who visited the Grand Lama in the Yellow Temple and reproached him for leaving the pure land of Tibet. The Tashi Lama is said to have listened humbly to the criticism.

There is too great a discrepancy between Porungheer's account in Captain Turner's book, and the Chinese records, and it cannot be denied that the latter are more credible.

The English account goes on:

Daily, countless thousands of the faithful streamed to the Yellow Temple. Imperial Princes, princes, high officials, monks, and the common people, thronged the gardens to receive his blessing, or at least catch a glimpse of His Holiness.

> "When any of the princes, or immediate relations of the Emperor, were presented they were received by the Lama without moving from where he sat, but they were distinguished by his laying his bare hand upon their heads while he repeated a short prayer or form of blessing. The nobility, or men of second rank, when introduced went through the like ceremony except that the Lama wrapped a piece of clean silk round his hand, and in that manner rested it on their heads whilst he repeated the blessing; and for those of inferior note, a piece of consecrated wood, of about a yard long, was substituted, and held by him in his hand, with the end of which he touched

their heads in like manner as he had the others with his hand." [1]

After five days the Emperor himself visited the Yellow Temple and was received with pomp and ceremony. His eldest son was ordered to show the Grand Lama all the palaces, temples, and other notable sights—even the ladies of the court were anxious to see him. He went to their palaces, sat on a throne, and blessed them in order of precedence. He sat bending forward, his eyes always lowered, so that he should not be contaminated by the sight of their beauty.

The Emperor himself took him to the Temple of Justice, and he spent a whole night in prayer with Chang-chia Hutuktu. Finally he was taken to the great Bell Tower, whose giant bell only rang out when the people were called to arms, or in thanksgiving for a great victory.

For several months the Emperor and the Prince of the Church exchanged many visits and officiated in the temples during services. On one occasion the Grand Lama returned to the subject of Warren Hastings; once again he bade the Emperor write to him and open friendly relations with him. The Emperor replied that he would willingly make the acquaintance of the Governor-General of Hindostan. The Grand Lama should dictate a letter and he would have it written, and he decided that the Lama should take it with him when he returned and send it to

[1] Op. cit., p. 465.

Warren Hastings in the manner he thought best. The Lama thanked him warmly.

If there is any truth in this account the Emperor was playing a part. He who, some years later, snubbed George III as if the latter were a disobedient vassal of the Son of Heaven, would never have lowered himself to enter into correspondence with the official of a Trading Company.

One day, despite snow and bitter cold, the Grand Lama paid a visit to the Emperor. After his return he complained of headache and fever, and the next day it was diagnosed as smallpox.

Everyone was upset. The Emperor hurried to his sick-bed with his cleverest doctors, and was himself weighed down with sorrow and anxiety. The Lama gave orders that alms were to be distributed to the faithful poor who prayed for him, and he joined in prayer with those around him. His last day had come.

What was the scene in that sick-room? Only with the help of imagination can we reconstruct it. In 1923 I visited the Yellow Temple, and the lamas showed me the room in which the Tashi Lama is said to have died. It was dilapidated and uncared for, unfit to live in. A piece of furniture like a catafalque stood along one wall. Now, that part of the Yellow Temple is a total ruin, and portions of it have fallen in. The few ragged monks who showed me round it in 1930 no longer knew where the death-chamber had been. (Pls. XXXI and XXXII.)

All the time the dying man must sit cross-legged, his hands on his knees, with the palms turned upwards, for he must die in the position of Buddha meditating on the way of perfection, and not in the position the founder of the religion assumed at the time of his death. On his death-bed, Buddha is always represented as lying down.

If the dying man was beyond helping himself, he was propped up upon cushions and pillows by his *chelas*. Ecclesiastics of exalted rank assembled round his bed, and the room echoed to their muttered prayers. Time after time they fell to their knees, the palms of their hands and their foreheads against the ground, in pious adoration of the departing spirit of Amitābha. The tired pilgrim who felt his life ebbing from him, whose only wish was to sink back against the soft cushions, was given no peace. The attendants replaced his fumbling hands in position; they supported his swaying head; they placed cushions under his elbows. Prayers rang in his ears incessantly. He seemed to listen. But in reality he heard no longer. His head sank to his breast. He was dead.

Then the monks were seized with the deepest veneration. They knew that Amitābha's spirit had now left the earthly clay in which it had lived for over fifty years. Through the change that had just taken place, Amitābha had manifested his power, his will, and his presence more tangibly than during the Grand Lama's life. They felt that a god was near. At the

LIII. Some of the Five Hundred Lohans in Lo-han-t'ang (p. 84)

LIV. A Lohan in Lo-han-t'ang (p. 84)

LV. Two jocund saints (p. 84)

LVI. The most stately temple in Shu Hsiang-szŭ (p. 85)

LVII. Shu Hsiang-szŭ: the pavilion (p. 89)

LVIII. Shu Hsiang-szŭ: a god riding upon a monster (p. 89)

LIX. The Temple of Confucius in Jehol (p. 92)

LX. The roof in the Golden Pavilion

very moment of death he had made known his intention of changing his place of manifestation. He was in the room. They seemed to feel his spirit brush past their foreheads. At any moment a miracle might happen, and the muttering of prayers rose once more, but now they were the prayers for the dead, no longer the prayers for a long life.

Once more Amitābha had begun his flight among the children of men. The great god was searching for a new-born boy in whose body he would find an earthly home. He floated over the *yurts* of the Mongols; the righteous heard the rustle of his wings among the Khalkha, and in the different banners of Ordos, Torgot, Alashan, and Tsaidam. As fast as horsemen could gallop, the news of the Grand Lama's death was spread abroad. Then all the people in Amdo, Tangut and Tibet, in Nepal, Bhutan, Sikim, and Ladhak hoped that the spirit would come to them, for, on the day the Grand Lama gave up the spirit of Amitābha, a boy child was born in one of those black tents or simple huts; there was a miraculous light in the sky and the new-born child spoke—it was the god speaking through his mouth. Word was sent to Tashi-lhunpo, and one day the holy conclave must decide which child had been chosen by Amitābha as his earthly resting-place.

In the death-chamber the monks busied themselves, seeing that the corpse stiffened in the right position. It must wear all the vestments of a Grand Lama. The yellow silk and gold brocade, the breadths of scarlet, the tall gold mitre; everything must be new and clean, and must never have been worn by a living person.

So the dead Lama was enthroned in all his magnificence, and prayers for the dead rustled around him.

The next day the Emperor arrived, tears streaming from his eyes, to pay the last homage to his departed guest. Like a confirmed believer in Lamaism, he fell to his knees in prayer and worship at the feet of the corpse, but deep in his heart he was laughing at the superstitions of Lamaism; he was a clever actor, and he knew well that the fame of his devout piety would fly round all the Lamaist lands, and would help to bind them still faster to the throne of his dynasty. His devotion, his tears, and his sorrow were moves in the game of political chess. The Emperor knew what he was about; he was a wise and crafty man, and the strengthening of the loyalty of the Tibetans and Mongols was well worth a Mass!

> "The corpse was immediately by the Emperor's orders put into a coffin, with great quantities of all kinds of spices and rich perfumes, and upon his return to the Palace, he gave orders that a small temple, in the form of those in which they deposit the objects of their worship, of pure gold, should be immediately prepared, large enough to contain the coffin when set upright; which after seven or eight days was, according to his orders, in readiness."

When it was ready, Ch'ien-lung again visited the Yellow Temple, attended by thousands of monks, and distributed vast sums of money among them, and among the Grand Lama's suite.

It was winter, and for two more months the Tibetan guests waited in Peking. One day the Emperor again appeared at the Temple and laid a lakh of rupees, (then about £11,000), brocade and silk, before the Lama as if he were still alive. He summoned the Tashi Lama's brother and told him that everything was ready, the season favourable, and he hoped he would have a safe journey back to Tashi-lhunpo. Finally he ordered the Tibetan to send fast couriers back to let him know when the soul of the dead man had taken up its abode in another body. He invited the brother to come back to China in person with the news.

Evidently Ch'ien-lung wished to control the spiritual succession in Tashi-lhunpo, and make the successor understand that one did not play an underhand game with the Governor-General of India, and escape unpunished.

The picture Father Amiot gives of the Tashi Lama's journey does not quite agree with that given in the English accounts. The latter seem to exaggerate the pomp which was displayed on the way to Jehol. Amiot's account also differs greatly from the Chinese official version already quoted. The source from which Amiot obtained his information was Ch'ien-lung's letter to the Dalai Lama giving him news of the Tashi Lama's death. Again the Emperor gives the impression that the visit was a surprise to him.

In his account, the learned Jesuit father tells of the different halting-places and of the gifts, though the latter are not so astounding as they are in the English version. He speaks of rosaries of pearls, saddles, ritual objects, palanquins, tents, standards and banners, and altar-bowls of silver and gold. At the banquet in Jehol, the Mongol Princes, chiefs of the different tribes, and the Korean and Mohammedan ambassadors, paid their homage to his Majesty.

In the letter alleged by Father Amiot to have been sent to the Dalai Lama, the Emperor does not mention the reverence they paid to the Grand Lama. But he does acknowledge his gratitude to the Tashi Lama for venturing on a journey of seven thousand miles for no other reason than to participate in the Imperial birthday celebrations. " With what emotion did I notice that he never once spoke of his return journey. He seemed to wish to remain near me." At the end of his letter the Emperor says that he has ordered the priests to recite the prayers for the dead for one hundred days. All the members of the Tibetan suite were given princely gifts, and the dead man's brother was invested with the title " Prince of the Effective Prayer."

The Emperor himself accompanied the funeral cortège on a part of its journey ; his eldest son went with it for three days, and two mandarins of high rank as far as Tashi-lhunpo in Tibet. His envoy carried a rosary of coral and a service of gold to the Dalai Lama.

There is reason to believe that, for political reasons, the Emperor received the Tashi Lama with almost incredible pomp, but that, in order to maintain his full majesty in the eyes of his successors, he gave orders to the historians and record-writers of the Dynasty which indicated quite clearly how near the truth they might go. Therefore the visit of the Grand Lama is included with the audience granted to all the other vassals, princes, and envoys on the birthday of the All-highest, and his death is passed over in silence.

The death of the third Tashi Lama may have been natural, or, as Abel Remusat and Koeppen assert, a political murder, but it can safely be affirmed that it came at an opportune time for the Emperor, for it served to strengthen a link in the chain of vassal states which, like a girdle of fortifications in the west, guarded the real China. But the annals might not speak of it. The game of big politics must be masked. Ch'ien-lung was a clever man, and he felt his responsibility for the safety of that boundless empire.

So the long procession left the capital of the Manchu Emperor.

Has there ever been a funeral procession in the history of the world to compare with it in splendour, magnificence, and variety? Doubtless Tamerlane's funeral procession from Otrar to Samarkand was an imposing spectacle for its time and, in barbaric greatness and warlike pomp, the last journey of Chingis

Khan from Ordos to Karakorum probably surpassed everything of its kind; but the funeral procession of the third Tashi Lama was, in its way, unique, not only on account of the dead man's power and importance as a prince of the church, but because of his intimate relations with the mighty Emperor Ch'ien-lung, and the tragedy of his fate.

The direct journey from Peking to Tashi-lhunpo involved a march of eighteen hundred miles. With the detours the funeral procession made, probably, two thousand four hundred. As the procession journeyed for seven months and eight days (the time taken by the flight of the Torgot) the daily marches were scarcely twelve miles, which, with so heavy a burden, was not bad going. In Tibet it had to cross passes over sixteen thousand feet high, ford mighty rivers when the snow was melting and they were swollen high and rushing furiously, and traverse waterless deserts and mountain ranges under the drenching rains and hailstorms of summer.

Yet we know nothing with any certainty of that wonderful journey, a journey unique in the annals of Asia. No one has described it. Thousands of men accompanied it, saw those fascinating camp scenes, and the whole of that colourful caravan, but no one has told what he saw. For the monks, it was a mourning procession, and all they longed for was the peace of their quiet cells in the monastery of Tashi-lhunpo; for the Chinese officers who composed the escort it was nothing but an order of the Emperor which had to be carried out; and, as for the rest, the majority could neither read nor write, and those who could, whether civilians, soldiers, or clergy, thought more about their horses and camels, their food and camping places than the funeral pomp that surrounded the dust of the Grand Lama.

We only know that the pyramid-shaped coffin was enclosed in a gold shrine, which, in its turn, was surrounded by a protecting shrine of copper, so that the bier must have been extremely heavy. It required a thousand bearers, who took turns at carrying.

Three days after the Emperor's decree that all was ready, the procession started from the Yellow Temple. It is quite certain that the start must have been witnessed by enormous crowds of people—we have already seen how the inhabitants of Peking thronged to the Tashi Lama to be blessed by His Holiness. Now, when he who was the Spirit of Amitābha had started out on a new pilgrimage, and the body of clay that had been his refuge on earth was being sent back to its own country, surely they would have wished to catch a glimpse of the bier that, for months on end, was to sway along over that barren country.

At the end of the first day's march, it was found that the burden was too heavy. The copper and gold shrines were taken off and, as a protection against wind and weather, the coffin was wrapped in oiled silk, and tied to the bier with breadths of yellow silk.

On leaving Tashi-lhunpo, the Grand Lama had been attended by monks of different grades, dignitaries, and an escort of fifteen hundred men. Possibly the escort had been left behind in Kunbum or Lanchow, after the Emperor's troops had joined the procession, but the clergy had remained with the Lama. Now the Tibetan escort was picked up, and the escort of two hundred horsemen provided by the Emperor probably returned when the Tibetan frontier was crossed.

For practical reasons the dead Lama must have gone back the way he came when he was alive. They travelled towards the west, keeping as far as possible in Lamaist lands, through Ordos and Alashan to Lanchow, Sining and Kunbum, following the Mongol pilgrims' road through Amdo and over Tang-la, and at last by Tengri-nor to Tashi-lhunpo.

Lighted by the spring sun, the procession passed through Sunit and Durbet, through the desolate country of the Ordos Mongols, past the tents of the Eleuts, between the rolling dunes of Alashan, where, time after time, sand-storms whirled up round the bier, and the holy emblems and the symbolic paintings fluttered in the wind. The golden figures of the gods, under their round canopies with hanging fringes, were blotted out and the bearers bent their faces towards the ground that they might not be suffocated by the flying sand. But on clear, calm days the images shone like gold, and the draperies, ribbons, and holy banners hung straight down against their poles, a billowing forest of the magnificent objects that belong to the cult of Lamaism. On black or white horses

LXI. The principal Temple at Ta-fo-szŭ (p. 82)

LXII. On the way home from Jehol

rode the monks, in yellow wooden hats, and robes as red as blood or as yellow as buttercups. The spears of the soldiers glittered in the sun, and their brightly coloured uniforms contrasted sharply with the yellow desert sand.

Behind the procession came countless caravans of camels loaded with chests, tents, grain, and all the hundred and one things that were necessary, led by Mongols on camels and Tibetans on horses.

What scenes must have been witnessed at those camping-places! Everything was carefully arranged. Round the Grand Lama's bier were the tents of the most important monks, set up in a square, while round the coffin stood altars bearing offering-bowls, symbols, and images. It was a perambulating mausoleum with watchers of the dead, guards of honour, and flaming lights in bowls of pure gold. All through the night prayers for the dead were droned over the departed.

The solemn, hollow resonance of long trumpets, the blast of conches, and the thud of drums rang out, and through the ceaseless mutter of prayers the six divine syllables *om mani padme hum*, were constantly repeated, the portentous *om* and *hum* long drawn out.

Round that mortuary chapel, multitudes of tents spread in all directions, with camp-fires burning before them, on which food was being cooked. The men were resting after the strain of the day. This was no noisy, shouting crowd, like the trade-caravans or soldiers on the march. There was an atmosphere of deep gravity. They were too superstitious to allow any open conviviality or drunken fighting. They were accompanying a Grand Lama on his last journey, and to have carried him would be reckoned as having acquired merit, when it was time for their next incarnation. After the fires had died down the stillness of the grave reigned over the whole camp. There was no sound but the barking of the nomads' dogs, the neighing of their horses and from time to time the dull braying of trumpets and the muffled thudding of the temple drums. Outside the boundaries of that city of tents was the majestic silence of the wilderness.

Wherever they passed, countless thousands of the faithful came from every direction to show the dead Prince of the Church the honour they would have shown him when he was alive. Chiefs and rich nomads appeared bearing gifts and there was never any fear that food for that vast escort would be lacking. It was considered an act of merit in the eyes of the eternal Buddha to show generosity to the dead Lama and his following; and there was blessing and good fortune for those who could press forward and touch the silk hangings of the bier.

In Kunbum, where the Tashi Lama had spent the winter, the funeral procession remained only for a few days while the coffin was placed in front of the image of Tsong-kha-pa in the Yellow Temple, where it shone dully in the red, smoky flames of the butter lamps. The abbots and priors and monks kept the death watch and mumbled the prayers for the dead in a monotonous sing-song. Pilgrims flocked in thousands to Kunbum from all the surrounding districts; a town of dark tents grew up round the monastery and, above that hurly-burly of horses, camels and tents, rose the temple buildings, with their golden, curved Chinese roofs.

The return of the departed Grand Lama was a triumphant procession, no less glittering and magnificent than his journey to Peking, two years before. The only difference was that the solemnity and festivity of the departure had grown more serious, and that his death had spread sadness over great tracts of country in Eastern and Central Asia.

The funeral procession left Kunbum and continued down that wonderful pilgrim's road that had been trodden by hundreds of thousands of Mongol pilgrims, whose goal was Lhasa or Tashi-lhunpo, untold numbers of whom had received a blessing from this dead Prince of the Church. Along that road a never-failing stream of silver had flowed into the treasuries of the monasteries and the big temple cities. Weary pilgrims had found renewed strength in the hope of seeing, at the end of the road, the two greatest avatars of Lamaism. The most pious had measured every foot of that road with their own bodies, stretching themselves full length, making a mark in the dust with their fingers, rising, and repeating the process from the mark, over and over again, until they reached the threshold of the temple. But none of them had made the pilgrimage after their death, like this Grand

Lama who was returning to his own monastery and his own grave. Over a hundred and twenty-seven years later I saw that splendid tomb, under its gold roof, and how the pilgrims from distant lands worshipped him, lying with their foreheads against the worn stones before his pyramid-shaped sarcophagus.

After the departure from Kunbum, the difficulties of the road increased. The procession had to ford the great Chinese and Indo-Chinese rivers in their upper reaches where there were no bridges ; but now it was autumn, the rainy season was coming to an end and, in the highest regions, the thaws had ceased. Between the rivers lay ranges of mountains which had to be crossed by high, difficult passes. Southwards from every ridge could be seen the next range with its saw-toothed or wavy contours, with chain after chain of snow-capped pyramids and cupolas sheathed in steel-grey, shimmering ice. In the passes, the procession was generally met by biting winds which swept the dry, fine snow-crystals in whirling clouds round the fluttering pennants and holy banners, round the eternally smiling Buddhas and the swaying bier, where the lonely dead sat throned, high in frozen majesty. When a snow-storm swept over the mountains the whole cortège was hidden from sight. Fainter and more ghostly grew the whole long procession. Only those close at hand were plainly visible, as they passed, shadowy figures in the whirling blizzard. Wild yaks, grazing in the protected valleys, ceased to feed, lifted their heads, snuffed, grunted and trotted slowly away. Antelope and wild sheep listened to their leaders' warning signals and sprang into the wind ; only the wild asses held their ground, interested and curious ; they pricked their ears, their nostrils widened as they snorted and ran forward to look. For hours they would follow the procession at a respectful distance, now in front, now at the side, now behind. With light, sure-footed step, and with the most graceful movements, they played with that slow, crawling host.

On some days the cool air was quiet and crystal clear. Then, in every direction, stretched vast wide vistas, unsurpassed in beauty anywhere else in the world. The slopes of the mountains shone violet, brown, and yellowish-grey, while their crests glittered with the white of eternal snow and the bluish-green of glaciers. Far away could be seen great herds of antelopes, perhaps containing as many as a thousand animals, whose long shining horns glittered like the bayonets of a marching army. Marmots whistled shrilly, and popped head-foremost into their holes. Bears, with a crescent of white fur round their necks, threw astonished glances at that dusky procession which moved slowly from pass to pass, filling the broad valleys and mounting up to the next ridge. In their nests on the crags sat the Golden Eagles, immovable, as if carved out of bronze, with great yellow staring eyes fixed upon that black snake which threatened their eyries. The setting sun was reflected in their eyes, making them shine like rubies. They saw the outriders come first, with horsemen armed with spears, swords, and bows and arrows following. They saw the red and yellow monks, twirling their prayer-wheels to the rhythmic muttering of *om mani padme hum*, half-asleep in their saddles; the sunlight reflected from the golden images; the standards and the temple banners casting long, dark shadows over the boulders and gravel. They saw the bearers, the poles across their shoulders, carrying the coffin which dominated the whole procession. With unwavering eyes they followed the long caravan of camels and horsemen which was still appearing over the distant pass in the north after the first mysterious shapes had vanished behind the ranges in the south. But the sun sank, the splendour died out of the eagles' eyes and their lids grew heavy. Twilight spread its veil over the mountain valley; the last camels strode past, and a new night dropped its pall of sorrow over the earth.

Month after month passed, and, at last, the turquoise-blue waters of Tengri-nor appeared in the south. On its further bank towered the glorious range of snow-clad peaks of the Nien-chên-tang-la. When they had crossed the dizzy passes they had not far to go to reach the Tsangpo river. There, lying in readiness, were great numbers of yak-skin coracles, but for all that, it took many days before the whole funeral procession was across. It was only one more day's march to Tashi-lhunpo. At last they swung round the corner of Shigatse-dsong and the monastery appeared, in all its splendour, at the foot of its cliff, the two mausoleums, with their golden roofs, rising out of the mass of white, red, and black buildings. One of them was quite new; it had been completed before the Grand Lama set off on his fatal journey to Peking. Now the grave-chamber was prepared and decorated with all the riches and splendour that had been rendered possible, thanks to the countless gifts which had been received on the journey to and from China.

When all was ready, the body of the Prince of the Church was placed in the *chorten* set with precious stones which still stands beside the north wall of the grave-chamber. One can well imagine the pomp and state of the Lamaist ceremony, but one can do no more than imagine it. Above the verandah-like entrance, with the Four Spirit Kings, a tablet bearing the name of the Emperor Ch'ien-lung in gold hangs to this day.

The memory of that dramatic episode in the more recent history of Eastern Asia lives only in a few ancient records. The temple-monastery of Hsin-kung still stands in its decay as a monument to that event; but before long its sanctuaries will have vanished, and its walls have fallen. The bells on the eaves will have rung its death-knell, and nothing but ruins will remain of the temple that was raised at the nod of an Emperor in honour of one of the greatest prelates of Tibet.

Chapter VII

K'ANG-HSI, THE FOUNDER OF THE SUMMER PALACE IN JEHOL

To describe in detail the labyrinth of summer houses, pavilions, pagodas, temples, parks, pools, and beautiful places which both the Emperors K'ang-hsi and Ch'ien-lung had built at Jehol, where they spent so many summers, is outside the plan of this book, which is concerned only with the temples. Our first duty on arriving in Jehol was to pay a visit to the Governor of the Province, General T'ang Yü-lin, which gave us an unsolicited opportunity of making a tour of that wonderful palace, so rich in memories, the scene of innumerable glittering entertainments, pompous audiences, court intrigues, love adventures, and the tyranny of eunuchs.

Here was the spot where the Emperors inculcated in the minds of the Mongol Princes the might and majesty of the Manchu Dynasty; here they honoured the Princes of the returned Torgot; here the Tashi Lama was overwhelmed with favours; and here Lord Macartney was shown that the King of England was nothing more than an insignificant vassal prince beyond the sea. Two of these historic events have been described already, and the following chapters will ring up the curtain on scenes and episodes which will show a fleeting glimpse of a beauty created by nature and art working in conjunction, and give some idea of what the Chinese culture of that time considered sublime and magnificent.

On the morning of June 29th, accompanied by Father Mullie, we drove up to the main gate of the beautiful park. The soldiers presented arms and, over the triple archway, flags were flying in our honour and that of the Republic. The whole of the forbidden city in Jehol is surrounded by a wall, over six miles long and sixteen feet high, made of stone and baked bricks, pierced in several places by gates.

A winding, stone-paved road led to a pavilion, where the Governor received his visitors. A large band was playing a European march. The General, a man of fifty-five, strongly built, and with a serious expression, simply dressed in a field-grey uniform, stepped out into the courtyard and welcomed us. He asked us to go into the reception room, in the middle of which stood a table covered with a white cloth, and four chairs, broad and massive as the thrones of emperors, covered with priceless old brocade. These were relics from the days of the Emperor Ch'ien-lung. Perhaps the Son of Heaven himself had condescended to sit in them and they had held the body that, on ceremonial occasions, occupied the Dragon Throne.

We were offered cognac, beer, lemonade, and cigars, and talked of our travels in Sin-kiang, Marshal Chang, and the reason for our journey to Jehol. The General assured us that we were at liberty to take measurements, sketch, and photograph as we wished. He would give orders that no one should disturb us. Finally, he commanded an officer to take us round the park and show us the famous sights.

We began with the main buildings and pavilions of the Imperial palace and admired the tastefully decorated throne-room, where the throne still stands, and where the walls both inside and out are of wonderfully carved wood, while the panels of the roof are all carved in different patterns. As usual, the pavilions were raised up on terraces about three feet high and the courtyards round them were paved with stone. As in the case of the temples, the effect was heightened by scattered groves of pines and firs.

The Copper Temple was a small sanctuary in the entrance hall of which four giant guardians, in coloured costumes, and armed with awe-inspiring weapons, faithfully kept watch. These were very well preserved. (Pls. XXXV and XXXVII.)

Then we walked up a long, gently sloping, stone-paved path to the foot of a hill at least three hundred feet above the level of the surrounding country. At its summit was a temple consisting of several small, neat pavilions which had formerly been very elegant, but were now almost completely ruined. From the highest kiosk, we could see to the horizon on all sides, and the palace park was spread out below us as on a map. We could see the irregular winding lakes, now dried up, which, in former times, had added to the charm and variety of the Imperial Park.

Near the kiosk was the palace wall, following the tops of the hills. The view was magnificent. We could see the Potala and Hsin-kung, with their temple buildings and green trees on the other side of the valley.

Finally, we glanced at the Pagoda, which was nine stories high, the lower ones being beautifully decorated in high relief.

In the *Handbook of Jehol* there is a somewhat sketchy description of the Summer Palace, with its various buildings, their places in the park, the positions of the hills, meadows and lakes, and the changing lights over the country in the red dawn and the evening twilight. We are taken to the Garden of Ten Thousand Trees and the Island of Fulfilled Desires; to the waterfall that seems to cast itself over a precipice of real jade, and, at its foot, breaks into countless pearls; and the rainbow bridges over the streams in the park. One pavilion, set apart for the use of the Dowager Empress, was surrounded by a park with ancient pines, under which storks flapped their shining wings (the pine and the stork are the emblems of longevity). There is a short mention of the audience halls, the open plain where victories over the people in the far west were celebrated, where illuminations were displayed, and races were held, and of the famous library with its priceless manuscripts now preserved in the National Library in Peking.

The period of Jehol's splendour was during the

reigns of the two great Emperors, K'ang-hsi and Ch'ien-lung, and reached its zenith during the sixty years when the latter occupied the Dragon Throne. Under the successors of Ch'ien-lung the importance of the Summer Palace declined, year by year, and ultimately died with Kuang-hsü, the last Manchu Emperor but one.

Then Jehol was one of the two centres from which the immense empire was governed. Those who are not familiar with the contributions of the two great Emperors to Chinese history may be interested to learn something about them that will throw light on their character and importance. They were the creators of Jehol, and a few words about them are therefore not out of place in this book. It is not my intention to treat the matter in any detail; there are more intimate sketches of them in the writings of de Mailla, du Halde, Amiot and other Jesuits who were missionaries in Peking during their reigns.

In brief, terse, and incisive words, Professor Bernhard Karlgren describes the period under which Jehol was created and flourished:

> "The three Emperors K'ang-hsi (1662–1722), Yung-chêng (1723–35) and Ch'ien-lung (1736–96) gave to China a period of prosperity and progress such as it had seldom experienced. In reality the first period of the Ch'ing Dynasty was, politically and socially, a new period of greatness, during which China, with a vastly increasing population and great economic development, grew into the enormous mass of people that became the centre of gravity of the whole of Asia.

" In religious matters there was not so much progress; intellectual and social life followed traditional lines, but, in all districts, there prevailed a care and precision, order and sense of responsibility which was in sharp contrast to the neglect, corruption, and decay of their successors.

" European accounts of China during the seventeenth and eighteenth centuries assert that material culture, agriculture, silk production, handicrafts in their great variety, the splendid roads, postal, and canal systems, as well as the administration and municipal enterprises, were at a height of excellence which put China in the foremost rank of the countries of that day.

" Emperor K'ang-hsi is among the noblest figures of the dynasty. Already, at the age of fourteen, he had grasped the reins of state, and for more than half a century he carried out a policy of enlightened government. Tall and stately, with a unique personality, he was at the same time a fighting figure who himself led his troops on arduous and dangerous campaigns, and the model of an accomplished monarch who was interested in the arts of peace. Simple and economical in his daily life, he could, on ceremonial occasions, splendidly uphold glittering pomp and circumstance. A wise and vigilant master of the vast machine of state, a hard worker, faithful to his duty, chivalrous towards his antagonists, unorthodox and independent as compared with the prevalent, petrified orthodoxy, himself a man of brilliant learning, an author, a fine poet, a never wearying patron of the arts, he was indeed a *roi soleil*. His son, Yung-chêng, lacked the greatness, probity and fine culture of his father, and as a hard, bad-tempered, suspicious and unscrupulous ruler, he made many enemies; but, even more exacting towards himself than he was towards others, ceaselessly active and efficient, he still kept China at its high level.

" The fourth Manchu Emperor, Ch'ien-lung, who abdicated after a reign of sixty years, in order not to exceed that of his grandfather, took the latter as his model, and was, like him, a monarch fortunate in war, and brilliant in the arts. His somewhat capricious and intensely vain personality lacked the flair of his brilliant grandfather." [1]

The following are some pronouncements concerning the founder and creator of Jehol, that have been taken from Chinese sources : [2]

" In June, 1689, the Grand Secretaries, the nine Ministers of State, and others presented a memorial to the throne stating that abundant rain had put an end to the drought in Shantung and Honan and that in Chihli the prefecture of Ta-Ming and the capital had had rain the day before. The Emperor had been offering up humble prayers for rain, respectful in the morning and vigilant at night, eating nothing but vegetables, and meditating for long periods. He was now quite exhausted and they begged him to take some rest for the sake of his health. The Emperor replied : ' We are not to be compared with other people. It is only right that we should be first to sorrow and the last to rejoice. On account of the persistent drought that has lasted for such a long period we have been filled with anxiety, and so have grown thin and lost our strength. Although we were not present in person at yesterday's prayer for rain, we have fasted with the deepest humility during each repetition of the prayer. Through the mercy of Heaven, rain has now fallen. When enough rain has fallen we may allow ourself some relief from care.' " [3]

In the first month of K'ang-hsi's 28th year (1689) the Emperor issued the following decree, which

[1] China, in Norstedt's *Världshistoria*, published by Sven Tunberg and S. E. Bring, Part 15 (Stockholm, 1928), p. 252.

[2] Almost all the following excerpts are taken from the work *Tung Hua Chuan Lu*. The translation was done for me by Mr. T. K. Koo.

[3] According to the theory of responsibility, the Emperor was answerable for all floods, droughts and pestilences.

demonstrates his goodwill and affection for his people :

"To the Governor-General and Governors of Liang Kuang.

"During our visit to the south we have ceaselessly thought of the well-being of the people and diligently sought to discover good ways and means of administration. Upon arrival at the districts of Su Chien in Kiangnan[1] we observed that the general conditions were more flourishing than upon our last visit. As we surmised that, although Kiangnan is our richest province, the extra taxes of the last years might have been too much for the people, we asked the Board of Revenue, before our departure from the capital, what was the condition of the Kiangnan treasury, and found that 2,200,000 taels had not been paid in. What we discovered by dint of questions throughout our journey only served to strengthen what we had already heard. Apart from the freeing of land from taxation, which we have already granted, we herewith remit all the remaining taxes on landed property, and all extra taxation. From now onwards the people are to be spared insistent collection of taxes, and the officials spared paying fines. You, Governors, shall carry this out unswervingly, so that all may actually enjoy this our benevolence as we intend. If anyone, for his own benefit, shall extort the outstanding taxes, he shall be severely punished. The people are the foundation of the land, and, if the people have enough, the kingdom is rich. We, personally, have always been very careful in our expenditure, and have never thrown away a thread of silk or a grain of rice. This has been because we desire to preserve everything to the advantage of our subjects, making them bear only the expenses of the state and the army. It is no light thing to remit taxes, but since the expenditure of the state during the last year has been less than the revenue, we can show our benevolence. Our wish is that wealth should accumulate among the people so that they can have all they need, whereby their morale may

[1] The Provinces south of the Yangtse.

be improved, and peace reign throughout the land. Herewith we command that this decree be speedily made known to all."

The same year and month, the Emperor issued the following decree to the Governors-general and high officials of Liang Kuang and Chekiang-Fukien. It shows the Emperor's taste for economy and his personal simplicity, in which his grandson differed from him so strongly:

" With the intention of investigating the grievances of the people, and to inspect the work of the officials in charge of the river, we have come to Kiangnan, and, as it is not far from there to Chekiang, we shall travel to that place to observe the customs. We have curtailed our Imperial state and are not using the state-carriage.[1] Our retinue will consist of little more than 300 persons.

" Lately, when we passed through the Yangchow district, the people had decorated all the streets and welcomed us warmly, filling all the main streets and the lanes. Although their intentions were praiseworthy we bewail the waste of money. We look upon all the inhabitants of our kingdom as our children, and if every family were well-to-do we should be quite happy without any triumphal arches. The towns through which we intend to go should take notice of our wishes and refrain from decorations. We saw how, during our welcome, the people, young and old, men and women, ran about in great confusion, fearing to be left behind, and thereby caused much noise and pushing. As our present visit is to be undertaken for the good of the people, we have not brought a large guard. But in crowds the good and bad are mingled, and it is our fear that some will be pushed down on the uneven roads, or else into the

[1] The expression 'state-carriage' includes the whole of the glittering pomp of the Imperial processions—banners, shields, state umbrellas, and other emblems of majesty.

water. If one should lose his footing we should feel sorrow in our heart. Hereafter the people are to kneel down by the wayside when they bid us welcome, and not walk about in disorder and give occasion for accidents. You are to make clear to the people our love for them and command them to obey us faithfully."

During the tour through Su-chow and Sungkiang, the nobility and the peasants of those districts offered all kinds of native products as gifts to the Emperor. The Emperor declared:

" Although all the state expenditure was covered by the people, during our tours in the south we have not made any requisitions from the people. But as, in your loyalty, you offered us these products of your land, we will accept one grain of rice and one fruit in appreciation of your zeal in making the offering."

Unlike his grandson, K'ang-hsi refused all valuable gifts which were burdensome for the people.

In comparison with the preceding dynasty, the Emperor K'ang-hsi maintained the greatest economy in his court and his personal life. In the first month of the 29th year (1690) the Grand Secretaries and other officials presented the following memorial:

" Some time ago, Your Majesty handed us a list of palaces, pavilions, and gates of the Ming Dynasty, together with a list of the (present) Imperial concubines, palace girls, and serving women, of Ch'ih Ning Kung, Ning Shou Kung, and Chien Ch'ing Kung, with orders that we were to read them and make a copy for preservation in the Yamen. We were also ordered to reckon up the yearly expenditure for palaces under the Ming Dynasty, as your Majesty wished to cut down expenditure on account of the drought, and had found it impossible. We have reckoned that Kuang

Lu Sze [1] during the Ming Dynasty spent 240,000 taels, while during the present year only 30,000 taels have been expended. Formerly 26,860,000 catties of firewood were used, but now the amount is only six or seven million catties a year. Formerly 12,080,000 catties of coal were used, now only one million. . . . Formerly there were 786 palaces, halls, pavilions and gates, but now the number is not one-tenth. . . . When the officials saw the lists, they all said that they had realized your Majesty's frugality, but they had not known any of the details. Since they have seen them, they truly understand that economy is being practised to the utmost. According to the Book of Rites, the Emperor has six Empresses, three Fu Jên, nine Pin, twenty-seven Shih Fu, eighty-one Yu Ts'i (concubines of different grades). In addition to these, who are the wives with titles, must be added thousands of palace-girls and serving-women. As T'ang T'ai-tsung, a good Emperor of the T'ang Dynasty, freed three thousand palace girls at one time, it is evident that there were still thousands left. Now, without counting Ch'ih Ning Kung and Ning Shou Kung, in Chien Ch'ing Kung (the Emperor's palace), reckoning from the Imperial concubines down to and including the serving women, their number is but one hundred and thirty-four, which is truly but a small number. Such a thing as that has never been known since the Three Dynasties, and even before the Three Dynasties it had never been equalled. The frugality and great virtue of your Majesty far exceed that of the past."

During his tour in the south in the 4th month of his 38th year, the Emperor gave an unusual proof of his enthusiasm for one of his predecessors of the fallen dynasty, in that he promulgated the following:

"Emperor Hung Wu, of the Ming Dynasty, was the founder of his line. Upon both our previous visits to

[1] The title of the Banquet-master.

the south we have, in person, sacrificed to him (in Nanking). The Grand Secretaries petitioned that, as the Emperor had twice sacrificed in person, this time he should send a high official on his behalf. The Emperor said: 'Hung Wu was a great and mighty Emperor not to be compared with ordinary emperors. Herewith I command that the Minister of War, Hsi Erh-t'a, shall make the sacrifices and we will personally offer the wine.'"

K'ang-hsi sympathized with other people's sufferings. In the 6th month of his 53rd year (1714) he issued the following decree:

"When we go over the frontier (the Great Wall) for the summer visit to the Jehol Palace, which has the reputation of being a cool place, we are still troubled by the heat. We think that it must be far worse in Peking. We are always mindful of the sufferings of our subjects. At the moment all under heaven is peaceful, the farmers and merchants are content. But we fear that the prisoners who are lying in prison, in chains or in the cangue, must be sick from the heat. When we think of them our heart is full of pity. We command therefore that all the prisoners in the prisons of the capital shall be treated with great kindness. More ice shall be taken to the prisons. The number of their chains shall be diminished and those who bear the cangue shall be taken out of it. When the summer has passed, the usual routine may be resumed. The Board of Punishments shall obey this our order, and comply with our desire to show the prisoners our grace, (even though) they have broken the law."[1]

The Emperor's thoughtfulness even embraced the horses serving with his army. In his 35th year he issued a decree wherein he emphasised the importance of not overburdening the horses.

[1] *Handbook of Jehol*, Part I, Chap. 1, p. 16.

" During military campaigns, the horses are a very important factor, and the soldier's baggage and equipment must be weighed, so that the loads are not too heavy and wearisome for the horses. . . . We consider that each soldier should have four horses. In a squadron there are four soldiers and one attendant for each soldier. The weapons, food and extra equipment of a squadron amount to nine hundred and seventy-five catties. Of the sixteen horses in a squadron, the soldiers and attendants need eight to ride upon, and each of the remaining eight should carry a load of one hundred and twenty-one catties. One mule is attached to every squadron, so that the standard of each animal's load should amount to one hundred and seven catties." [1]

It is a well-known fact that the Emperor was very interested in scientific investigations ; especially those of an astronomical or mathematical character. To this fact the writings and the activities of the Jesuits in Peking bear witness. K'ang-hsi was proud of his accomplishments and was always ready to seize any opportunity of instructing his ministers in the secrets of nature. To judge by the following episode from the 4th month of his 31st year (or May, 1692), he was not so well versed in astronomy.

He was talking with his minister K'u Lê Nu and some other gentlemen, in Fên Chih Yüan, or the Garden of Abundance.

[1] All military operations, plans of campaign, the establishment of bases, and the details of transport, were prepared with the greatest accuracy. The military experts gave lectures before the Emperor. We are told that these officers had to be careful what they said, or they exposed themselves to the Emperor's criticism and to detailed questions that they themselves had often never thought of. Once the Emperor asked how many horses and camels could be watered at one time at a certain well in the Gobi Desert.

" The Emperor asked if they had noticed his rice when they passed through the garden. They said that they had noticed that it was already a foot high, and that they had never seen such growth so early in the year. The Emperor told them that, when he first planted rice, he selected the kind that is ripe for harvest in the 7th month, and so his rice was ripe in the 7th month. That is why it was already so tall . . . the climate in the north and south is different, and so are the seasons. If one district became warm before or after another, it was on account of their distance from the sun. Therefore it was of the greatest importance to compute the degree of latitude. In order to fix the north and south it was absolutely essential to take, as the standard, the height of the sun at mid-day. Not even a compass was infallible. If there happened to be any iron object near by it would attract the needle, and the result would not be accurate. . . . K'u Lê Nu asked how it was that in Heilungkiang the days were so much longer and the nights were never really dark. The Emperor answered that Heilungkiang lay in the north-east ; that the sun rose and sank in the north-east, therefore the nights in Heilungkiang were short and, even after sunset, it was never quite dark."

The Emperor's sense of responsibility was coupled with the greatest judgment and a legitimate belief in his own sound powers of discrimination. This appears very clearly in the following decree to the chamberlains and others issued in the 1st month of the 29th year (1690):

" In affairs of state we personally do our utmost to find out what is right or wrong, never throwing the responsibility on others. For example, when the insurgent Wu (San-kuei) was banished (to another part of the Kingdom) So-E-Tu presented a memorial requesting that the person who propounded that scheme should be executed. But we abided by our own judgment, and ordered banishment.

"At that time military operations were being carried out in thirteen provinces for several years, and during the whole period we ourselves bore the responsibility for all those great matters. Can you remember one case in which we laid the responsibility upon you? A few years ago, the soldiers in the Hu Kuang provinces mutinied. At that time there were much discussion and many different opinions, but we said that the affair was not serious. We sent down the Green Banner soldiers and they quickly suppressed the mutiny. Again, in the matter of Russia, both Manchu and Chinese officials said that the distance was too great to allow of an action being successful, but we insisted that the matter should not be left undecided, and sent officials to the border. When they had followed our instructions, Russia submitted. We have not boasted of our successes; but, with you, whenever you have had some slight success, there is someone to trumpet abroad your fame. We, the master of all, are only afraid that some among the millions (of our subjects) may be discontented. The criticisms of the ignorant do not trouble us in the least."[1]

What the Emperor thought of the Great Wall as an effective defence for China proper, is shown in a decree in his fiftieth year, issued on the occasion of a petition which Ts'ai Yüan, the Commandant of Ku-pei-k'ou, made to the office of works, concerning repairs being done to the Great Wall at Ku-pei-k'ou pass.[2]

"In his memorial, the Commander Ts'ai Yüan shows himself entirely ignorant of affairs. In the management of the state, Emperors have to follow certain fundamental principles. They cannot merely put their trust in strategic

[1] *Handbook of Jehol*, Part I, Chap. 1.
[2] Op. cit.

points for the protection of the kingdom. Since the Great Wall was built in the Ch'in dynasty, it was repaired during the Han and T'ang dynasties, yet can one say that those dynasties did not suffer from invasions from across the border? Our T'ai Tsu (august ancestor, the first of the Manchu line) led his great army, and entered the land without meeting with any resistance. It is clear that, in order to hold the kingdom, the Emperor must exercise virtue and enable the folk to feel contented. When the people are cheerfully submissive, the foundation of the empire has been laid, and the frontier is naturally secure. That is what is meant by the proverb: 'Collective purposes build a fortress' (Union is strength). We have visited Ku-pei-k'ou and Hsi-fêng-k'ou and know that, in these places, most of the Wall is falling into ruins. If repairs are to be undertaken now, can it be done without injury to the people? Then, too, the Great Wall stretches for several thousand *li*, and how many soldiers would be necessary to guard it? Ts'ai Yüan has not realized this, and therefore what he says is quite valueless. The Nine Ministers are hereby so informed."

Some days before issuing that decree, according to the Tung Hua Chuan Lu, the Emperor, returning from Ku-pei-k'ou, said:

"The Ch'in dynasty built the Great Wall, but, by conferring favours on the Khalkha Mongols, our dynasty prevailed upon those (tribes) to take over the defence of the northern border, and they are more impregnable than the Great Wall."

In these wise and eloquent words the Emperor gave the key to the whole of his Mongolian policy, and explained, briefly and succinctly, a principle that was afterwards followed and enlarged upon by his grandson.

In the same pregnant sentence we also find the key to Jehol, the Summer City, which he founded outside the Great Wall in order to have the Mongol Princes under his eye, so that he could impress them by splendid audiences, dazzling hunting expeditions, and awe-inspiring military manœuvres, and that he himself might occupy the northernmost outpost as a protection for his immense kingdom.

But in the records he wrote concerning the founding of the Summer Palace in Jehol, he took care never to mention a word of his true political reasons. In these records, sprinkled with outbursts of poetry, he almost asks his people to forgive him, the Ruler of the World and the Son of Heaven, for allowing himself the luxury of building a Summer Palace outside the borders. We may be quite certain that it was not done for his own pleasure and well-being, or because he had a passionate love for the country round Jehol, but from motives of clever statesmanship and far-sightedness. In order to mask his real intentions, he sought an outlet in a dreamy and attractive poesy, and, to justify himself to his critics, who might perchance accuse him of neglecting his duty, he explained that Jehol was so near Peking that he could be at his post in the capital in a couple of days. The record runs :

"(Jehol) where Chin-Shan (the Gold Mountain) rises, where the warm springs run, where the clouds spread out over valleys through which trickle brooks of clear water, where rocky pools and verdure abound, where the rivers are broad and the grass luxuriant, yet no damage is done to farmsteads, where the breeze is clear and the summer cool, suited to rest and relaxation. Jehol is indeed a spot created by nature for her children.

" Many times have I visited Kiangnan (the district south of the Yang-tse-kiang), and I prize the loveliness of its scenery. I have been twice to Shensi and Kansu, and I am familiar with the kingdoms of the west. I have crossed the Dragon Sands (the Gobi Desert) in the north, and in the east I have travelled through the Long White Mountains. The grandeur of the rivers and mountains and the honesty and simplicity of their people cannot be described in words. But I have not used them (i.e. not chosen any of these places for the site of my country Summer Palace).

" Jehol is near the Celestial Capital. To reach it takes no more than two days. It is a wide expanse of lonely country. The choice of this district cannot encroach upon my duties. In harmony with the natural contours of the country, I have built pavilions in the pine groves, thereby enhancing the natural beauties of the hills. I have made water flow past the summer-houses as if leading the mountain mists out of the valleys. To create such beauty is beyond the power of human skill. It is the gift of nature itself, and causes no expense of carving beams or painting columns.

" With my love for the sublime peace of the forests and springs, I can calmly watch the creatures, the waterfowl playing on the blue water, not fleeing at the approach of men ; the deer going in herds in the evening light ; the eagle circling in the sky or the fish leaping out of the water, one high and one low, according to the laws of nature ; and I can also enjoy the purple distances, or gaze at the vault of heaven which sometimes seems near and sometimes far above me.

" Whether I am wandering about enjoying the view, or resting, my mind is always upon the harvest. Neither day nor night do I forget the lessons of history. For the encouragement of cultivation I pray constantly for full baskets ;

for the sake of good harvests I rejoice at the blessed rain which falls at an auspicious time. That, in general words, is a picture of my life in the Summer Palace in Jehol.

"When I find pleasure in orchids, I love uprightness; when I see the pines and bamboos, I think of virtue; when I stand beside limpid brooks, I value honesty; when I see weeds I despise dishonesty. That is what is meant by the proverb 'the ancients get their ideas from objects'. It must ever be remembered that all an Emperor has comes from the people. Not to love is not to understand this. Therefore I have written this that I may remember it day and night, and remain always upright and reverent."[1]

Already in 1677 K'ang-hsi had had a little country seat built in Luan-ping.[2] Every year he visited Jehol, but his first palace in the town in the land of the Harchin Mongols was not erected until 1703. Doubtless he found that the fresh air benefited him, and took pleasure in hunting among the surrounding hills. During the following years several more pavilions were built, and when the foundation year, 1711, arrived, there were thirty-six "beautiful places" or beauty spots, to each of which was given a poetic (four-syllabled) name. "The Cypress Wind with the Ten Thousand Crypts" was one, and was that of a hall on a steep slope beside a lake. "The Hundred Slender Cypresses ward off the surrounding Sunbeams: their rustle is like the sound of Flutes and Bells" was another. "Surrounded by Clouds and Mountains" was a pavilion on the crest of the highest hill.

"Its top soars among the Clouds and touches the

[1] *Handbook of Jehol*, Part I, Chap. 22, 11A–12A.

[2] According to Franke, op. cit.

Milky Way. The Hosts of the Mountain greet it. Many hundreds of miles lie stretched below it like an outspread screen."

On the road from Ku-pei-k'ou to Jehol, and from Jehol to the hunting-grounds at Mulan, in the north and north-west, K'ang-hsi built ten or more small summer-houses or rest pavilions, where he spent the nights, or partook of refreshment on his journeys or hunting expeditions. For such purposes, naturally beautiful valleys were chosen, with shady trees and purling brooks like the one we found for our halt on the road to Jehol, although nothing remained of the lovely elegance which, according to contemporary sketches, was to be found even in those small summer-houses.

During his summer visit to Jehol the Emperor divided his time between various occupations. He hunted tigers, antelope and deer, held military manœuvres in order to follow the knightly and war-like traditions of his ancestors and to keep himself, his generals, and sections of the Manchu army in full vigour. He received the Mongol Princes and envoys in audience and presented them with gifts and titles of honour. But first and foremost, even from the Summer Palace, he ruled his kingdom with an iron hand. Sorrow and worry did not pass him by. His numerous sons were a pack of scoundrelly good-for-nothings, or dissolute, vain, irresponsible madmen who, during his later years, caused him constant anxiety for the future of the kingdom.

The son who succeeded him and, as the Emperor

Yung-chêng, ruled China for twelve years, was in many respects a remarkable man, but lacked all his father's great qualities. Yung-chêng seems to have had almost an aversion for Jehol, and no place in the Summer Palace is associated with his name.

His free hours, and they certainly were not very many, the Emperor K'ang-hsi devoted to the study of China's history and literature, and he himself wrote freely, both prose and verse. When he was working thus, for himself alone, he found a refuge in Shui Fang Yien Shiu, a group of palace buildings with 15 rooms on the farther and more secluded side of one of the islands, surrounded by mirror-clear waters, and with a stone balustrade along the shore. A Chinese writing says: "There the Emperor K'ang-hsi found time to study, even upon days that were so full of work. In the central hall hung a tablet with the characters Fêng San Wu Ssŭ . . ."

Perhaps it was in just that peaceful spot—a Chinese Dar-es-Salaam—that one of the greatest military figures of the time, wearied of the hard campaigns and the clash of weapons round the borders of his kingdom, wrote this song in praise of Jehol:

> "O high mountains, that fall towards the green hills,
> O blue streams, lapping against the steep cliffs,
> See, the fish calmly follow your steps, and play,
> And the storks sit enthroned on the tall trees.
> See, the monk cannot reach the distant grotto,
> And strangers go astray in the cool forests.
> But I have always loved this spot,
> And I am alone with my heart's desire."

CHAPTER VIII

CH'IEN-LUNG'S COURT AT THE SUMMER PALACE

THE sixty years during which the Emperor K'ang-hsi's grandson occupied the Dragon Throne mark the last glorious period in the annals of the age-old Empire of China.

It is not my intention to sketch the personality of the Emperor Ch'ien-lung, or the history of China during his long and happy reign. In the following chapters, glimpses of his character and personality will appear here and there, for the episodes and events that are described in them often concern the last great Manchu Emperor. But, in order to give some idea of him, the opinion held of him by those capable of judgment, and of the political rôle he played, I shall give two short quotations.

Backhouse and Bland, in the following extract, which gives their summing up of the Emperor's character, certainly exaggerate on some points :

> " Ch'ien-lung ascended the Dragon Throne at the age of 25, in 1736, and reigned over China for sixty years, at the end of which cycle he abdicated in favour of his son, Chia Ch'ing. Judged by the verdict of his contemporaries,

and of posterity in his own country, as well as by the evidence of European observers, he was beyond question the ablest administrator and the wisest ruler that China had known for several centuries. By his government, as well as by his successful wars in Sungaria, Central Asia, Burmah and Tibet, he completely restored the prestige of the Manchus which his predecessor had seriously undermined. In his private life he appears to have been distinguished by qualities of sincerity, broad-mindedness, and courage which alone suffice to raise him far above the level of his predecessors and successors. He was impulsive, it is true, intolerant of failure in those upon whom he conferred high authority, especially in military affairs; superstitious and naturally ignorant of China's relative place and power amongst the nations, but gifted nevertheless with clear insight, sweet reasonableness, and a highly sympathetic nature. He combined in his person to a high degree the best qualities of the soldier and the statesman, but was besides a scholar, a historian and a poet. In his domestic life also he was successful in maintaining his parental authority, while preserving the respect of his sons and grandsons; a polygamous autocrat in his relations with women, he was neither uxorious nor luxurious. After a reign of unexampled success, he left the Empire stronger and more prosperous than it had been for several centuries." [1]

About the Emperor's private life, the same authors say:

"In his private life, and in the administration of his household, Ch'ien-lung combined a high sense of his Imperial dignity with frugal habits. Throughout his long life he retained his devotion to the chase, for the wilds of Manchuria and Mongolia, for the simple open-air life which had

[1] *Annals and Memoirs of the Court of Peking*, 1914, p. 310. The authors of these words have possibly been too much influenced by the judgment of the Jesuits, which, for obvious reasons, is thoroughly panegyric.

made his forefathers the hardy men they were. It would be interesting to study the coincidence between the decay of the Imperial hunting parks, the decline of manly exercises amongst the Manchu aristocracy with the gradual ascendency of the eunuchs, that begins definitely to assert itself in the reign of Ch'ien-lung's successors."

"As the head of his family and the Palace household Ch'ien-lung exercised a very strict supervision over his domestic affairs until old age and the increasing affairs of state combined to relax his energies in this direction. In private as in public life the secret of his success lay in personal attention to detail, indefatigable energy, a broad mind, and a personality in which a strong sense of order and discipline combined with many sympathetic qualities. Ch'ien-lung was essentially a statesman, but he was also a good sportsman. As the traveller gazes to-day on the melancholy ruins of Yüan-ming-yüan, and the hunting parks at Jehol and Peking, he cannot but wonder that a race which could produce so wise and so virile a ruler, and send its armies half across Asia, should to-day be represented only by the besotted and effeminate creatures who walk so delicately and uselessly as Manchu Princes."[1]

After having described the war in Central Asia, Professor Bernard Karlgren continues :

"The whole vast territory that had formerly been under the Eleut Khans on one side, and the Islamic Princes of Kashgar on the other, was now made into a real Chinese province, with Chinese *Ambans* under a Governor in Kashgar, and strong garrisons in all the important localities, such as Khotan, Yarkand, Kashgar, Aksu, Kucha, Kuldja, Kobdo, Urumchi, etc.

"The prestige of China in Central Asia grew so great that for some years even potentates west of the Tarim lands,

[1] Op. cit., p. 330.

in Ferghana and Afghanistan, sent tribute to the Emperor of China, as they had been in the habit of doing during that period of greatness, the T'ang epoch. At last the great programme of conquest by the Han and T'ang Dynasties had been realized.

"With unparalleled vigour the Manchu Government carried on its great policy in other directions as well. After a bitter war in Burma (1765–9) the Burmese king acknowledged the suzerainty of the Emperor and sent yearly tribute.

"Long and extremely expensive wars in south Ssŭch'uan, and in Kueichow against the Miao-tzŭ, succeeded, in 1775, in subduing the independent inhabitants of those wild mountain tracts who had never before submitted to Chinese authority. Expeditions against Annam towards the end of 1780 strengthened China's influence over that country, and finally, when the Gurkhas of Nepal made a raid into Tibet, in 1790–1, General Fu K'ang-an marched, with a Chinese army, up into the Himalayas, drove the wild tribesmen from one inaccessible strong point to another, and finally followed them down the frontier of India. Again the Emperor of China was incomparably the strongest and most powerful man in Asia."[1]

That a policy of conquest of such dimensions could not be carried out by any other than a despot of remarkable ability, cannot be denied. The Chinese of our day, who pronounce such hard and derogatory judgments on Ch'ien-lung, forget that he was the last Emperor who succeeded in holding China at the height of her power and prosperity.

Father Amiot, in one of his letters, tells of all the strange things the Jesuits had to make to amuse the Emperor and to win his favour. If they were cleverer than all the others, the Emperor would find them

[1] Norstedt's *Världshistoria*, Part XV, p. 258.

THE EMPEROR'S BIRTHDAY BEING CELEBRATED IN THE STREETS OF PEKING

indispensable, and their position, and that of their mission, would be safer in China.

Father Chalier constructed a wonderful watch, and Fathers Benoist and Castiglione invented the most amazing fountains. Brother Thibault made a mechanical lion that could go for a hundred steps, and Father Sigismond an automatic man. When the latter was finished, the Jesuits feared the Emperor would say: "You have made this man, and taught him to walk. Now teach him to speak."

Nothing had to be impossible. The Emperor was the Son of Heaven, and for him everything was possible. "Moreover," Father Amiot says, "his taste changed like the seasons. At one time he had a craze for music, at another for art, painting, architecture, fountains, or what-not. We must ever be on the watch, for it is always the Jesuits who must explain the wonderful things from Europe."

In everything Ch'ien-lung took his famous grandfather as his model. In his edicts, decrees, and memorial tablets, he constantly refers to his 'august grandfather, the Emperor.'

It was quite natural that, in his love for Jehol, he should follow in K'ang-hsi's footsteps. But he even went further still, and did not shrink from spending vast sums on the temple-monasteries, of which some have been described in the preceding chapters, and the thirty-six summer-houses, pavilions and 'beautiful places' that, like K'ang-hsi, he built in the park of the Summer Palace. He gave his new buildings names of three characters, as poetical as those of his ancestor. He enlarged and beautified the spot, made lakes with artificial islands and arched bridges, brought the most priceless collection of objects of art that could be found throughout China to the new palace, and added rare manuscripts and books, illustrations and maps, to the Summer Palace Library. In a word, he made Jehol a pearl among the towns of China, and it is said that, in riches and rare and precious objects, it competed with Peking. On the way from Ku-pei-k'ou to Jehol, and from there to the hunting preserves of Mulan, he added three more to the already existing rest-pavilions and hunting-lodges.

Ch'ien-lung's buildings are described in the *Handbook of Jehol*, but the descriptions are dry and uninteresting. It will be enough to devote a moment's attention to the pagoda of nine stories. It belonged to the Yung-yu-szŭ temple, the 'Temple of Eternal Protection' which was built in 1751 and contained a record tablet in Manchu, Chinese, Mongol and Tibetan, in which the Emperor, after warmly praising that mountainous country which was so conducive to quiet meditation, continues, according to Franke :

> " When, as a boy, I was allowed to come here, with my Imperial Ancestor, I wandered about, peaceful and happy. It was no time of rest, yet it was a rest. In that abandonment fraught with blessing, earth and heaven melted into one. More than thirty years have passed since then, and again I rest here after the autumn hunting. The cypresses and clouds are as they were, and the beams of the halls still soar into space. But I remember the changing genera-

tions in my house; benefits received I will reward, and I will pray for grace, and therefore, in my summer residence, beside the Garden of Ten Thousand Trees, I will build a sanctuary that shall bear the name of the Eternal Protection. Here shall not only the bell, the fish, and the litany (ritual objects in Buddhism) help to proclaim the honours of this beautiful residence, but the suns of my Imperial Ancestors shall not set for a thousand autumns, and children and children's children, officials and people, shall believe that they wander here for all eternity. It shall be a sign that Śâkyamuni, Gridhrakûta, and Vajrâsana rejoice in the protection of the Heavenly Dragon (the Emperor)."

The pagoda itself caused the Emperor considerable trouble. According to the record-tablet, he wished to build it after the models he had seen on his visit to the south—possibly in Su-chou or Hang-chou. But the builders of the north were not used to that technique, and their work collapsed. After some years, perhaps after architects had been called in from the Yangtse provinces, the pagoda was completed in 1764. The Emperor always declared himself a Buddhist, but now, in an outburst of candour, he admitted on the record-tablet that he was no believer in Buddhism. He continues:

"My opinion is that we should not believe the idle talk about the eight earth symbols which govern fortune and misfortune. Thereby we shall only excite the people's credulity. . . . It is my intention that coming generations shall see from this tablet that in honourable feats of war I have followed the example of my forefathers, and spread fear and veneration, and that a constant propagation of the doctrines of Buddhism has not been my paramount object."

The Emperor K'ang-hsi had written an apology for his building operations in Jehol, therefore Ch'ien-lung too wrote, but not till he was advanced in years, a kind of apology:

" It was in the year Hsin-mao (1711) that my grandfather the Emperor completed the thirty-six scenes (beautiful places) in the Summer Palace of Jehol, and it happened that I was born in that same year. What cause and effect lies in that coincidence is incomprehensible. After my accession to the throne, it was not till the year Hsin-you (1741) that I began hunting in the autumn. Arriving at the Summer Palace, I wandered about, slowly and reflectively, thinking of it with love.

" But as my Imperial Grandfather has already written all there is to say of the Summer Palace, why should I write?

" Yet I was born in the same year as the Summer Palace. For the first time I waited upon my Imperial Grandfather (i.e. accompanied K'ang-hsi upon a hunting expedition) in the year Jên-yin (1722). Now a cycle of sixty years is accomplished, and once again it is the year Jên-yin (1782). What I have kept hidden deep in my heart for all these years should now be set forth clearly, and proclaimed as a reminder to my descendants of that which I myself was reminded of.

" When I visit the Summer Palace, I daily venerate Heaven. I obey the precepts of my ancestors, and work for the welfare of my subjects, and subdue and bring to peace people both far and near (i.e. make the frontier peoples feel their loyalty through audiences and other proofs of my favour). These points have already been written down time after time in my poems and prose compositions. Have I possibly still some weighty thoughts that have never been expressed?

" My Imperial Grandfather built the Summer Palace as a means of ruling and pacifying the frontier peoples. His enthusiasm for simplicity and his love for economy stand out clearly from the pages of the royal document. His designs were far-reaching. Although, during the thirteen years of my Imperial Father's (Yung-chêng's) reign, no hunts were held, he gave the following instructions :—' That I did not go to the Summer Palace in Jehol, and did not take part in military exercises at Mulan, because I had so much to do and because I am by nature comfort-loving and hate the spilling of blood, is altogether my own fault. My successors should follow the example of my Imperial Grandfather (K'ang-hsi), and carry out military training at Mulan. Do not forget our family law.' I myself, my brothers, and my privy counsellors listened to this enlightening instruction. All these are now no more, and, if I do not set it down, the holy wish of my late Imperial Father will never be known to posterity.

" Since the Han and T'ang Dynasties, pleasure palaces and country parks have been built by every dynasty, but carrying out the caprices of these rulers was only a waste of money and work. In extreme cases, this led to the fall of the dynasty. Such cases should be taken to heart as warnings, and should not be imitated.

" But the Summer Palace at Jehol lies outside the frontier (the Great Wall). The reason for its construction was to emphasize the art of war, not to honour literature.

" As for the high mountains, the steep cliffs, the water and forests, the wandering storks and deer, the soaring eagles and the playing fish, the buildings in the shadow of the precipices, the pavilions beside the brooks, the luxuriant grass and the ancient trees, they have a natural beauty that makes one forget worldly cares. Compared to the pleasure palaces and country parks of the Han and T'ang Dynasties, there is not a single point in which [the Summer Palace] does not hold its own. To abandon myself to its beauties and forget all else would be to change the Summer Palace I have built in the land of the goat-smell into a snare, and cause me to do a wrong to my ancestors. . . . Now that I am old I must speak out."

Truly, Jehol, the Imperial City, abounding in memories, is unique. How melancholy it is to wander through the scattered parks of Pi-shu-shan-chuang, and listen to the echoes of its vanished greatness. If those little ruined pleasure palaces, those romantic pavilions and silted pools, silent water-falls, shattered bridges and 'beautiful places' could but talk, what would they not have to tell? Matters of State, domestic politics, frontier politics, magnificent banquets, and drunken orgies, military manœuvres, hunting parties, sports, love affairs, an unbroken succession of changing romances, jealousies, quarrels between concubines, intrigues of mandarins and princes, generals and eunuchs, entertainments, picnics in the parks, fire-works, audiences to princes and envoys from all the countries of Asia, one glittering carnival of constantly changing pageantry throughout the reigns of the two greatest Manchu Emperors.

What little information we can find about Jehol in Chinese records is painfully meagre and colourless. We have already seen how poorly the contemporary annals treated the visit of the Tashi Lama, though it was an occurrence to which the Emperor attached the greatest importance. As we shall see, the visit of the English Ambassador in 1793 was treated in even more cavalier fashion. No real account of the great, colourful, historic entertainments is in existence; all that exists is a brief dry record, without life, pith, or fantasy. The descriptions of the ceremonies follow the Book of Rites which imposed the same traditional etiquette on all the Emperors of the dynasty.

The account of Ch'ien-lung's visit to Jehol in his twenty-eighth year (1763)[1] merely says that the Emperor accompanied the Dowager Empress on her journey beyond the Great Wall. She stayed in the T'ang Ch'uan palace and the Emperor in Shih Ch'ao. "The Emperor issued a decree that, on account of the last year's floods, the taxes in the districts through which he was to travel were to be reduced by at least one-half." The Emperor, who arrived first at Jehol, went out to meet the Dowager Empress.

One day he issued a decree in which the commandant, eunuchs, and military guards in the Summer Palace were rewarded. On another day he dined with the Dowager Empress in the Chüan-a-shêng-ching palace, and for seven days he entertained the visiting princes, important civil and military officials and the Mongol princes to tea and fruit.

Upon his birthday he went to the Dowager Empress's palace to perform the usual ceremony. After that there were the ordinary audiences and receptions. Then it was time for the yearly autumn hunting in Mulan, a district to the north of Jehol. The name is Manchu and means "hunting roe-deer". The district seems to have been well wooded and watered. One would imagine that a tiger hunt in which the

[1] *Handbook of Jehol*, Part I, Chap. 18, 14B–17A. All the following excerpts from the Chinese Handbook have been translated for me by Mr. T. K. Koo.

Emperor killed a tiger a day for three days might well have provided the material for a colourful and sensational record, but no. Such and such a day the Emperor stayed in a certain hunting pavilion, 'hunted and killed a tiger', and that is repeated word for word three or four times, only the name of the pavilion and the date are different. Otherwise there is nothing to say but: 'The Emperor hunted and killed a tiger.' As to how the hunt was organized, what weapons he used, whether he rode, how the tiger was driven or surrounded, not a word.

But from the same Chinese sources (Part 1, Chap. 26) we can obtain a detailed account of the inexorable rules laid down for the autumn hunting in Mulan. This account is very interesting, and, with the help of imagination, we can picture to ourselves the incredible machinery that was set in motion every autumn when the Son of Heaven set out on the famous hunt.

"RITES TO BE OBSERVED ON SETTING OUT FOR THE HUNT."

"An edict announcing the hunt at Mulan is to be sent out beforehand, that the necessary preparations may be made. When the edict has been sent out, the official guide shall proceed with his soldiers along the road that the Emperor is to take, to give orders to the local authorities to hold themselves in readiness. The various boards and bureaus shall send a memorial to the Emperor asking him to name the princes and high officials who will accompany him. The Eight Banners shall send a memorial to the Emperor asking him to appoint the Captain of the Guard. The Bureau for Vassal Administration shall order the Dzasak princes and others to hold themselves in readiness to accompany the Emperor on the hunt.

"The day before the expedition sets out, an official shall be sent to the Hall of the Ancestors (Fêng-hsien-tien), to announce the autumn hunt. Upon the day of starting, the Emperor, in hunting dress, riding on a horse, shall leave the palace accompanied by a body-guard and officials riding before and behind him. As upon the Emperor's visits to the provinces, the officials shall wear full court dress and kotow when they say farewell to the Emperor.

"Upon his arrival at Jehol, the Emperor shall stay in the Summer Palace till after the Mid-Autumn festival. Then he shall set off for the hunt. Before the start, the Minister of War, who also serves as the leader of the hunt, the officers in attendance and the guard, proceed to the park and humbly wait there.

"When they have reached the hunting reserve, the Captain of the Guard, officers, and soldiers, select the place where the tents are to be erected. The tents must be strictly guarded and no one shall be allowed to wander about during the night. The disobedient shall be punished according to the law. At a distance of about two *li* from the tents, sentries shall be posted.

"Every day, at the 5th night watch, the high official in charge of the hunt, accompanied by the Mongols (beaters), shall go to form the cordon of beaters. No one else is allowed to go outside the sentry-posts. When dawn breaks, the Emperor sets out from the Imperial tent and goes to the watch-post (a smaller tent on the outskirts of each park) to watch the formation of the cordon of beaters, composed of 1,250 Mongols. In the middle of the line is displayed a big yellow banner, called in Manchu, Fo-leh. The hunters take up their positions in two wings and spread out in the prescribed manner.

"The one on the extreme left shall carry a white banner, the one on the extreme right a red one. At the head of each party there shall be a blue flag. When they approach one another, and the circle is almost completed, the foremost ones ride quickly, carrying their banners. When they are almost meeting at the 'watch-post' they shout '*ma-la-ha*' and the cordon of beaters is complete.

"The Emperor, carrying a quiver, bow and arrows, comes out of the 'watch-post' and steps into the circle of beaters where the wild beasts are. The Emperor shoots, and then he commands the officers and guards to shoot. Every animal that escapes from the cordon may be hunted and shot by the officers and soldiers. The names of those who shoot down any animals are entered in a register. If there is any dangerous beast, such as a bear or a tiger, the head-huntsman sends guards to the 'watch-post' to inform the Emperor of this fact, whereupon the Emperor rides to the place and orders the tiger-hunters (with guns) to shoot it, or the Emperor himself fires the 'wonderful gun' and kills the beast immediately with his bow and arrows. If there happen to be too many deer within the cordon, it is broken on one side to give some of them an opportunity to escape.

"At three in the afternoon the hunt comes to an end. The Emperor returns to the Imperial tent, where the spoils are counted and presented to the accompanying officers and princes. When all the hunts of the year are at an end, the Mongols are sent home to their various tribes. The Emperor returns to Peking by way of Jehol."

Here follow in the Chinese records, "Specifications concerning the Imperial Tent" drawn up in Ch'ien-lung's twentieth year (1755).

"The Emperor's travelling tent shall be square inside and round outside. The place (for the erection of the tent) shall measure 206 feet by 174 feet, and shall be furnished with yellow hangings for walls. (The camp is known in Chinese as 'The City of the Yellow Curtains'.) Outside the City of the Yellow Curtains, at a distance of 180 feet on the east, south, and west, and 150 feet on the north, a wall of nets shall be erected, hung upon yellow ropes. There shall be 166 nets, each 6 feet high and 8 feet wide. Inside this enclosure 175 tents shall be pitched. This is the Inner City. Over the three main gates, big banners are raised. At the east gate a red banner with yellow edges, over the west gate a yellow banner, and over the south gate a white banner (all of satin). Round the Inner City there shall be set up 41 big pennants. There are also nine guard tents.

" Outside the Inner City is the Outer City, consisting of 250 tents, pitched on a belt of ground 120 feet wide. There are four main gates . . . and four watch tents. To the east of the Outer City shall be placed the *yamens* of the cabinet, the six boards, etc. If there is not room to accommodate them, they (the surplus) may be placed in the south.

" At a distance of 600 feet are 40 watch-tents . . . The city of tents is strictly guarded, and surrounded by tents like the stars (in the sky).

" The Emperor's tent stands within the City of Yellow Curtains. It shall be 20 feet high and 34 feet across. The high tent-roof shall be supported by 160 bamboo poles. The tent walls shall be 5½ feet high, with the front and back doors 4½ feet high and 2½ wide. In the middle is placed the Imperial throne which shall be 1·65 feet high, 3·95 feet deep, and 5·75 wide. On each of the two side walls shall hang a sword, a quiver, and a musket.

" On the open square in front of the Imperial Tent, two round tents shall be raised, one on each side. . . . Behind the Imperial Tent shall be erected a square tent, which leads into a tent-hall 2 or 3 rooms wide. . . . The horizontal tablet shall bear the inscription ' Szŭ-i-chih ' (always ready for residence). The side rooms shall be provided with windows. Behind this tent three round tents shall be pitched.

" The kitchen, dining-room, store tent, etc., shall be placed outside the City of Yellow Curtains."

The Rites give the most detailed instructions for building the Imperial Tent City, and the plan and grouping are those of the Forbidden City in Peking. When the Emperor went out on the autumn hunting in Mulan, he had to maintain a great deal of ceremony in order to receive, with fitting state, the Mongol princes and chiefs who came for audience.

The Rites also set down the personnel that was to accompany the Emperor on his hunting expeditions.

> " When the Emperor goes to Mulan, the chief-guide, accompanied by the corps of guides, sets out from Ch'ien-ching-mên ; their duty is to keep the road clear, select camping places, and set up the tents.
>
> " The Chief of the Imperial Life Guard, accompanied by three superintendents, start us off with the baggage, etc., packed on carts. There are 2 officers and 15 soldiers for the baggage ; 3 officers and 24 soldiers for the three great banners ; 1 officer and 8 soldiers for the pitching of the Imperial Tent ; 8 officers and 80 soldiers to supervise the pitching of the outer tents ; 2 officers and 30 soldiers to answer for the Mongol sentries ; 4 officers and 100 soldiers posted to the guard tents in the Inner and Outer Cities ; 19 officers and 190 soldiers for the guard tents ; 8 officers and 140 soldiers as general guards for the whole ; 2 officers and 20 soldiers for the commissariat ; 2 officers and 8 soldiers to cut the grass ; 1 officer and 15 soldiers for the three flags, and a company of 'Tiger-hunters' consisting of 2 commanders, 2 head-huntsmen, 2 assistant head-huntsmen, 160 hunters, and 40 apprentices. When the Emperor proceeds to the hunt all these should be at their posts."

The Park guards :

> " There are 800 soldiers from the eight Mongol banners. In K'ang-hsi's 45th year (1706) there were only 101. In

Yung-chêng's 12th year (1734) 90 were added. In Ch'ien-lung's 18th year 609 were added. The guards are selected from among the Manchu and Mongol soldiers by the Commanders of the Eight Banners. Every guard has 120 *mow* of land. But in the north, and in the Hing An Mountain region, every guard has three milch cows, a bull to every thirty cows, and thirty sheep, because it is too cold to cultivate the land."

The ceremonial at the banquet that the Mongol princes gave in honour of the Emperor began as follows:

"When the Emperor went to Mulan to hunt, it was usual for the princes of Cho-so-tu and Chou-wu-ta to give several public and private banquets in his honour. In order to decrease the expense, the Emperor Ch'ien-lung ordered that only one banquet should be given. For this banquet they shall provide 6 Mongol tents, 18 white camels, 18 saddle horses, 162 unbroken horses, 18 cattle, 162 sheep, 81 casks of wine, 27 tables of food, 20 wrestlers and tumblers, 20 expert riders, and 250 circus horses. The princes shall report, in advance, to the Bureau for Vassal Administration, concerning the banquet, and deliver a list of the names of the Mongol Princes, dukes and others, at the same time asking that one of them shall be selected to offer wine to the Emperor. On the appointed day, the Bureau of Armaments shall humbly set up the Mongol tents. The camels, horses, cattle, and sheep, shall be kept on the left side of the road which leads to the Imperial City of Tents."

Then follows a description of the ceremonial at the banquet, the rules of drinking, the time of the meal, and the entertainment afterwards.

In order to show his practical nature, and his fatherly interest in the people and the cultivation of the soil, the Emperor—who was given to making theatrical gestures for outward effect—often issued decrees that were obviously intended to appeal to the populace. Here is one from his 25th year (1760), which is in the *Handbook of Jehol*, Part 1, Chap. 2.

> "The land round the Summer Palace (in Jehol) has always been reserved for our retinue, and no cultivation is allowed there. So it must always be while we visit the district. But to let the land lie fallow for the whole time would be a pity. As our visit to Mulan always takes place in the autumn, grain can be grown and harvested before our arrival. If our visit to the graves of our ancestors should take place in the spring, the autumn grain could be sown. If the visit takes place in the autumn the spring grain will have been harvested already. It is accordingly ordained that the Minister of the Imperial Household shall divide the newly surveyed ground round the Summer Palace between the officers and men who guard it. The land shall lie idle when we pass by it, but it may be ploughed afterwards. In this way the land will not lie fallow, and, in addition, it will be a great blessing to the soldiers."

How the Emperor Ch'ien-lung honoured the Mongol Khans and the other princes and envoys who were received in audience, is described in the records of the Bureau for Vassal Administration, Chap. 31. These audiences took place in the Garden of Ten Thousand Trees (Wan Shu Yüan), in the park of the Summer Palace in Jehol. It was upon such a ceremonial occasion, which coincided with the Emperor's birthday, that Lord Macartney was present. We have to realize that it is almost impossible to imagine a more complicated banqueting ceremony, especially where drinking the Emperor's wine was concerned.

A STREET SCENE IN PEKING

Possibly the unhappy men who were present for the first time had to go through a course of rehearsals before they appeared before the Son of Heaven.

" When the Emperor orders that a banquet shall be given to the khans, *bei-leh* (princes) and other noblemen, together with the Hutuktu lamas,[1] in the Garden of Ten Thousand Trees, the Bureau of Armaments (a bureau attached to the Imperial Household) sets up the large Mongol tents and hangs up the yellow curtains. In the middle of the tent is placed the Emperor's throne. On both sides of it, slightly to the back, are to be placed long divans for those of the Hutuktus whose rank entitles them to sit on low divans. Other Hutuktus sit at the sides beyond the Leopards' Tails (the Imperial Guard). The Inner and Outer Dzasak, the Torgot and Durbet Khans, *bei-leh* and other noblemen sit on cushions to the right and left, in order of precedence.

" Upon the entrance of the Emperor, conducted by the officiating masters of ceremonies, the Hutuktu lamas, clad in embroidered dragon mantles with plain long jackets, and the khans, wearing the embroidered dragon mantles beneath jackets with breast-plates, fall to their knees outside the tent and greet him. When the Emperor has taken his place on the throne, the Hutuktus, khans, and others are conducted into the tent, where they perform the kotow ceremony once, whereupon they go to their places.

" The head cup-bearers enter to serve tea. When the Emperor drinks, all fall to their knees in their places and kotow once, remaining on their faces until the Emperor has finished his tea. The Imperial Life-guard then serves tea and all receive it on their knees. After another kotow they all resume their places.

" Now the draperies in front of the side-tables are drawn aside. The Master of Ceremonies steps forward to the cup-table, and walks to the middle of the tent reverently

[1] Living Buddhas ; manifestations of some quality of Buddha.

bearing in both hands a wine-jug, the Emperor's goblet, and a cup of gold. All rise. The Master of Ceremonies goes forward to the side-wall of the tent, and stands facing the west. He pours wine into the Emperor's goblet. The wine-bearer, who has been chosen from the Mongol princes beforehand, first goes out of the tent to take off his jacket, then he returns and kneels, turning towards the Master of Ceremonies. All fall to their knees. The Master of Ceremonies kneels, still facing the west, and gives the Imperial goblet to the wine-bearer, whereupon he rises and steps backward. The wine-bearer rises and walks down the middle of the tent facing the Emperor, but turns aside and kneels on the west side of the Emperor's throne. He offers the Emperor wine ; the Emperor accepts it, whereupon the wine-bearer rises and withdraws to the place where he received the goblet, going along the western side. Here he kneels. The Emperor drinks, while the wine-bearer kotows and so do all the rest. The wine-bearer rises and passes down the west side to the throne and, kneeling, receives the Imperial goblet. Then he passes down the centre back to his place where he kneels. The Master of Ceremonies steps forward, kneels, and takes the Imperial goblet from the wine-bearer and withdraws. Now the rest rise. The Master of Ceremonies pours wine into the gold cup and enters. Standing, he holds out the cup to the wine-bearer, who continues to kneel. He receives it, kotows once and drinks the wine. The Master of Ceremonies takes the cup and withdraws. The wine-bearer kotows again and goes out of the tent to put on his jacket. He returns, goes to his place, sits down, and all the others sit. The Emperor eats and presents delicacies to the guests. The chief butlers enter with trays of dishes. The Emperor eats meat and offers it to all. When the meal is ended, the cup-table is carried into the tent and Mongol musicians come in and play. Wine is carried in to be offered to the guests. The princes whose right it is to receive wine from the Emperor are led forward and kneel humbly, while the Emperor himself pours out wine for them. The others are served wine once by the Imperial Guard under the supervision of the adjutants-general (of whom the Emperor has four). Those who have received wine from the Emperor withdraw to their original places and kotow, the rest follow their example. When they drink wine they kotow once more. The Mongol music ceases. Picked men from the Imperial corps of wrestlers enter to compete with Mongol wrestlers. After the wrestling bouts, acrobats enter to display their skill. When they have finished they withdraw. The table in front of the Emperor is removed. All kneel in their places and perform the ceremony of the three kneelings and nine kotows. While the guests kneel with their faces to the ground the Emperor withdraws."

The ceremony for celebrating the Emperor's birthday in Jehol was as follows : [1]

" At the fifth watch, on the Emperor's birthday, the Bureau of Imperial Equipage shall have the Imperial carriage in front of Tan-po-ching-ch'êng tien. The eunuchs will arrange the Middle Harmony Corps orchestra under the eaves on both sides, while the Red Throne Great Orchestra is placed inside the door. Under the porticos on both sides of the courtyard, places have been arranged for the officers, facing towards the north. The Emperor's sons, princes of the blood belonging to the first six grades, and the Mongol princes should be placed below the steps of the *Tien*, divided into right and left columns ; officials of the second rank and higher (are gathered) outside the courtyard gates, those of the third grade and lower, according to rank, outside the gate of the Summer Palace. When the water in the hour glass has almost run out (early in the morning) the officials gather in their various places, wearing embroidered dragon robes and jackets with breastplates, and humbly wait.

[1] Ta-Ch'ing Tung-Li, Chap. 16.

"At the appointed time the Minister of the Board of Rites requests the Emperor to come to the *Tien*, wearing the dragon robe and *Kun* jacket. (When he has arrived and seated himself) the Harmony Corps orchestra plays. Three fire crackers are set off. The great orchestra plays. The Emperor's sons and all others perform the ceremony of the three kneelings and nine kotows, as directed by the marshals. At the end of this ceremony the Minister of Rites informs the throne that it has been performed. To the music of the Corps of Harmony, the Emperor withdraws. Officers of the Court of Ceremonial conduct the officers out in order of precedence.

"The chief eunuchs invite the Emperor to come to the Inner Court to receive congratulations. The Empress, in Dragon Mantle and long Dragon coat, stands directly in front of the Emperor (who sits) and the Imperial Concubines stand a little way behind her, on both sides, all clad in embroidered robes. They perform the six *Su*, the three kneelings, and three profound bows (with the right hand touching the ground). During this time the Great Orchestra plays. After this ceremony the ladies are conducted back to their several palaces, and the Emperor withdraws."

In the *Handbook of Jehol*, Part 1, Chap. 2, there is a decree of Ch'ien-lung's 44th year (1779) concerning the traditional birthday ceremonies, and the visit of the Tashi Lama, which gives a fleeting glimpse of the Summer Palace in Jehol. In it we are given some idea of the Emperor's fondness for travelling. On his visits, not least in the Yangtse provinces, he received the homage of his governors, officials and subjects, and nothing pleased him more than the pomp and state, and the adoring, humble jubilation of the common people. These visits were a great delight to those districts through which he travelled, and the people, though they had to bear the expense, were certainly flattered by the gracious visits of their Emperor. Once, a very old official of high rank advised the Emperor to desist from his visits south, because 'the murmuring of the people filled the air'. The Emperor angrily ordered him to give the names of those who were murmuring. The official had to say that it was impossible to mention them by name, whereupon the Emperor replied: "But I can name countless numbers who have begged me to come."

The decree reads as follows:

> "In an earlier decree, issued in reply to the memorials from the Governors-General and Governors of Kiangnan and Chêkiang which stated that the people of these two provinces requested that we should come and inspect the river and sea dykes, we have already declared our intention of choosing a fortunate day in the first month of the year Kêng-tzŭ (1780) for the start of our tour in the south. Concerning that part of the memorial which deals with our seventieth birthday falling next year and states that they wish to celebrate it in the districts we are visiting, we have decided positively that this must be forbidden. Thinking that two extremely fortunate events would happen one after the other, events at which all would rejoice—for our own seventieth birthday falls in the year Kêng-tzŭ, and our august Mother's ninetieth birthday in the next year, Hsin-ch'ou (1781)—it was our original intention to allow all to present their sincere good wishes. But now that our original intention cannot be put into effect, I have not the heart to give any festival of homage. But bearing in mind that our scholars and beloved subjects have for several years been hoping for some favour, we have issued an edict that examinations are to be held both in the country and in the capital, and that in accordance with universal desire, all the

provinces in rotation shall be freed from the taxes on rice and beans.[1]

"When, next year, we return from the south, after having sacrificed at the Altar of Earth, we shall go to the Summer Palace in Jehol. As usual, the birthday celebrations will take place in the eighth month.

"If we remained in Peking to receive congratulations, we think that our mind would be more troubled (at the thought of our mother) and therefore we wish to go to the Summer Palace. The Panchen Lama's petition to be granted an audience, that he may present his good wishes, is a very auspicious event and we have given him permission to come, commanding him to appear at the Summer Palace. We are not going there in advance merely to receive his congratulations, but are doing it for the sake of his convenience. Fearing that the officials at the court and in the provinces will not rightly understand our thoughts, and therefore still intend to send us memorials concerning festivals of homage, we wish them to understand that such would not only not provoke our favour, but would increase our troubles. Is it in this way that courtiers should venerate and honour their Emperor? Upon our eightieth birthday we will allow all officials to present their good wishes and render us homage at their discretion, but this time it must not be. For the rest, on our sixtieth birthday, Ku-pei-k'ou and Jehol were bedecked with lanterns and coloured silks, which we did not like. Next year such things should be strictly forbidden."

Within the intimate circle of the court, the Emperor, to enhance the pleasure of a feast, would himself take a part in some play. Once he entertained his mother on her birthday by summoning the best company in Peking to act before Her Majesty and the court. Suddenly, he disappeared from his place in the

[1] Only in eight provinces were such taxes levied.

audience and, after a time, appeared on the stage, painted, bearded and in costume. He played a solo-rôle, the aged Lai-tzŭ, in one of the twenty-four examples of children's love for their parents, the cardinal virtue in China. Lai-tzŭ, at the age of 80, had both parents still alive and, in order to make them forget their great age, he behaved towards them as if he were still a little child.

Now the Emperor was seen to imitate him, and come creeping up, on all fours, to the front of the stage. Before his mother's seat he rose, and began to play with a toy drum, and two balls on a string, which made the drum sound when he rubbed it from side to side with his hand. He made comic faces, dancing, and leaping about. The Dowager Empress was delighted and sent the most lovely lady of her court on to the stage with a present of sweets crying, "A reward for the aged Lai-tzŭ." The Emperor kotowed, and thanked her for the great honour.

In the year 1751 the Emperor journeyed towards the south and took his mother with him.[1]

In Kiangnan, or the Provinces south of the Yangtse, the wealthy salt merchants played a very important part. It was to them that the Governor-General, or Viceroy of Kiang-su and Chêkiang, turned with the request that they should finance the Emperor's journey which, otherwise, would be an enormous

[1] The following story is taken from a modern romance, founded on tales of the court that have been handed down, which Professor Ferd. Lessing has translated for me.

burden to the people. Foremost among the merchants was Chiang Hao-ting. He possessed a bamboo garden of great beauty, and there gave daily theatrical performances with his own company of actors.

As the Emperor was coming the rich merchant had his garden decorated, and the best actor, who was also a clever singer and dancer, learnt many new songs to sing to His Majesty.

A certain rival in the salt trade, Wang Yü-lung, had no sleep after he heard of the other's preparations. He had a troupe of actresses, the loveliest in the land. Among them was the fourteen-year-old Hsüeh-ju, or Snow White, who was more beautiful in colour than the river nymphs. This troupe Wang Yü-lung placed at the disposal of the Viceroy.

Countless junks and boats were brought up the quiet waters to Ch'ing-chang, where a number of important officials were to receive the Emperor. In answer to the Emperor's inquiry as to where his august mother could reside, the Viceroy answered: " In the bamboo garden of Chiang Hao-ting." The great lady was conducted there but, in the afternoon, she returned to the Emperor's junk. When, the following morning, Chiang Hao-ting came down to the wharf in the hope of having his reward, both he and all the officials were told that they might not go on board the ship. His Majesty must not be disturbed. The junk was hung with heavy draperies of yellow silk. From its interior came the joyous voices of a choir—all through the night they had

THE EMPEROR'S PALANQUIN BORNE BY TWENTY-EIGHT MEN. IT IS SURROUNDED BY OFFICIALS. THE PALANQUIN STEPS ARE CARRIED IN FRONT.

been singing for the Son of Heaven—and they still sang.

The next time Ch'ien-lung visited the south, Wang Yü-lung again won the favour of the Emperor by his fairy-like pageantry. When the Imperial junk arrived at the harbour, where countless officials lay with their noses in the dust, the Son of Heaven noticed a peach, as big as a little house, which seemed to be hanging from a tree, and was exactly the same shape as an ordinary peach, the symbol of longevity.

Suddenly a gong boomed inside it; the peach fell of its own accord and rolled down to the edge of the water. The Emperor sat silent, astonished. Again the gong boomed, the peach opened and from it fell a vase of noble shape and proportions. Its name was '*p'ing*' (calm, peace, health), and it signified thanks to the Emperor who had given those advantages to his people, and a wish that they might continue to attend him.

Out of the vase rose an artistically cut tablet, bearing the character *shou* (long life), and at the same time five bats flew up, *fu* (bat) symbolizing the five different kinds of good fortune that were desired for the Emperor. In the twilight they fluttered round the vase, then suddenly vanished. The Emperor expressed his delight. But now his attention was caught by another scene. It was announced that Hsi Wang-mu, the royal mother of the west, ruler of the Land of Fairies, was approaching. One after the other, the famous eight genii appeared, played by the most lovely women the Emperor, a connoisseur of women, had ever seen. With beautifully trained voices they sang a poetic song in which a description of the beauty of the bewitching landscape was skilfully interwoven with praises of the Emperor.

Suddenly a cloud was drawn over the scene, on which stood Snow White, the Queen of Fairyland, more beautiful than ever. Slowly, solemnly, she stepped out of the cloud and went towards the front of the stage, surrounded by the eight genii, and now from nine fresh young throats rang out a song in glorification of the Emperor, his boundless tenderness, and his care of his land and people.

Charmed with what he saw and heard, Ch'ien-lung had to restrain himself from leaving his seat and hurrying towards those fairy princesses.

Even at court ceremonies which did not lack a certain political significance, the Emperor would indulge a daring sense of humour. The following anecdote is told of the Eleut King, Amursana, who had come from far Dzungaria on a visit to the court in Jehol. When King Galdan Tsering died, there was a fierce struggle for the succession between the members of his family. Vanquished by his rival, Davaji, in 1754, Amursana hurried to complain to the Emperor and beg for his help.

China was enjoying a period of peace and the Emperor was devoting the whole of his time to beautifying the Summer Palace in Jehol. New fairy palaces and pavilions were springing up round the pools in the park, decorated with a luxury never before seen in the Middle Kingdom. In one of the rooms, among other priceless objects, was a screen, with a carved jade of the T'ang Dynasty, representing the Emperor Ming-huang at the moment of falling off his horse. The war-like Manchus could think of nothing more contemptible than an Emperor who had not a sure seat in the saddle, and who could not control a horse.

Possibly the Emperor was thinking of this jade when a courier reported that Prince Amursana had arrived at the border of the land of the Chakhar Mongols, and, accompanied by other noble horsemen, would shortly be at court. To his chief-secretary, Lai-pao, the Emperor said:

"The godless scoundrels in Dzungaria are fighting among themselves: that Amursana is coming to give himself up is a gift from Heaven. The opportunity shall not be lost."

The devoted court official answered: "For your Majesty's shining virtue, only a rattle of drums is needed to annihilate the rebellious princes."

The prince came and was received with honour in the Garden of Ten Thousand Trees. At the banquet, high spirits prevailed and Amursana boasted loudly that as a mounted archer he was the best in all Dzungaria. The Emperor sent a cautious word over the table to Lai-pao, ordering him to bring out a wild, unmanageable stallion. Then he said to Amursana, jestingly: "Give us a proof of your skill in the noble art of horsemanship."

Prince Amursana rose and swung himself nimbly into the saddle. The wild stallion bucked like a steel spring and the Eleut prince, in all his finery, rolled in the dust of the park. This touched his honqur, his life itself. There sat the Son of Heaven, surrounded by all the highest persons in the land, laughing. Amursana sprang into the saddle again and, for a second and yet a third time, landed on his back.

"What wonderful horsemanship! That horse must evidently be an enemy of man!" the guests said mockingly.

Amursana was shamed in the eyes of those present, and when, the next day, he left Jehol, there was no halo of glory round his head. But the Emperor tempered justice with mercy and helped him to the Eleut throne. There he showed a faithlessness that was to cost him dear. The very next year, 1755, he massacred the Chinese garrison which the Emperor had established in Kuldja. Whereupon the brave general Chao Huei drove him from the kingdom.

Amursana had much to regret when, for the last time, he saw the tops of the Tarbagatai Mountains vanish in the south, while the endless desolation of Siberia spread its silent forests round his fleeing feet.

The following decree, issued in the eighth month of Ch'ien-lung's fifty-sixth year (1790), is of quite a different kind, and both amusing and interesting.[1]

[1] *Handbook of Jehol*, Part I, Chap. II, pp. 26B, 28B.

" This year we reached the age of eighty-one years. The harvest is good and the rain fell at the right time. The day before our birthday a light rain fell but the next day the sun shone. The sky was clear as crystal and the weather was ideal. In truth this was a favour from Heaven. On the eleventh day we invited our sons, grandsons, great-grandsons and our great-great-grandson to take part in an archery tournament at the Hill Palace. Our great-great-grandson, Tsai-hsi was only eight years old, but he was able to hit the bull's eye three times out of five. We were very pleased, and bestowed on him a yellow jacket.

" This reminded us of how, many years ago, we accompanied our grandfather (K'ang-hsi) to an archery contest at the Hill Palace. Five times in succession we hit the bull's eye. We were honoured by his kind praise, and (our grandfather) rewarded us with a yellow jacket. At that time we were twelve years old, while our great-great-grandson, although he is only eight, can already hit the bull's eye time after time. We think of the blessings of Heaven, the fruits of our ancestors' good deeds, and the other blessings which have fallen to our lot.

" We have passed our eightieth year and our great-great-grandson is already old enough to study. We calculate that, if we reach our ninetieth birthday, we shall be in a position to see six generations together, bringing their good wishes, all in the same hall.

" We dare not congratulate ourselves on this great and diversified good-fortune ; on the contrary, we will strive to do our best, working hard day and night, honouring Heaven, and constantly turning our attention towards our duty in the interests of the people, so that we may be deserving of Heaven's favours.

" When our great-great-grandson was born, an event seldom recorded in history, we ordered the governors of our provinces to search out and verify all the families in which there were five generations, and when these were reported to us we especially rewarded them. In the past we served our Imperial Grandfather (K'ang-hsi) and the departed Emperor, our Father (Yung-chêng), and now we have a great-great-grandson. We have seen seven generations. Such a great felicity is still more extraordinary. Herewith we order our Commander of the Eight Banners (and others) to make inquiries as to whether, among our subjects, there are others who have seen both their grandfather and their great-great-grandson. Those who can show proof of having so done are to be brought to us. We will honour them with rich gifts and, together with them, we will celebrate the great age which we have attained."

That this promise was not an empty one is proved by a letter from Father Amiot, written in Peking on the 15th of October, 1785.[1]

From the different provinces came word of 192 families, the heads of which had seen five generations of descendants. Four of them were over 100 years old.

"The Emperor has sent them all magnificent gifts in accordance with their social status: all of them belonged to well-to-do classes. In addition to the gifts, which were alike in all cases, he sent special presents to the four centenarians. The Emperor himself composed verses in their honour, which he wrote with his own hand and had delivered with due pomp and ceremony, and he gave each of them permission to erect outside his gate a '*tablet*' upon which the verses were engraved."

The Emperor also gave a banquet for them, at which he himself was present, and to which the Jesuits, Amiot, Carme, Bourgeois and Espinha were invited. The reception took place in a big courtyard in the

[1] *Mémoires Concernant les Chinois*, Vol. XII (Paris, 1786), pp. 509 *sqq*.

Palace of Peking. Three thousand old men were present. They sat on mats, four to each table. When the Emperor arrived, they all rose ; he was attended by his sons, grandsons, and great-grandsons. The meal was substantial, mutton with sauce, roast duck, chicken, and pork. The Emperor wished every dish to be emptied, and the old men were given the same wine as His Majesty. The princes went from table to table, and pressed the old men to eat and drink. The Emperor's eldest son was so energetic that he might have been taken for a harassed steward.

The wine was served in porcelain cups. " The Emperor desires that each one shall take home the cup from which he has drunk at the feast, and that each may live long to use it and, every time he drinks from it, he shall remember this day and what it stands for."

Musicians played, and then the actors came in. They had masks both before and behind so that their backs should never be turned to the Emperor or the guests. They acted a play about old age and the passage of the years. Then eunuchs sang, their voices shrill and penetrating. At the end, the ministers and officials distributed presents. To a few of the guests the Emperor himself handed gifts. They received purses embroidered in gold and silver, lengths of silk, sceptres of sweet-smelling wood inlaid with pieces of jade and the emblem for " May everything happen according to your desires ", staffs of cedar decorated with dragons' heads, the character '*shou*' (longevity) in silver and, finally, the Imperial verses. "To the venerable old men who have been bidden to a feast, to rejoice me by the memory of what my august ancestors once did upon a similar occasion."

The Emperor Ch'ien-lung loved literature and poetry, and the temples and palaces of China are overflowing with proofs of his ability as a poet. They have seldom achieved any high degree of fame, but have generally been stigmatized as inferior. Malice insists that the best of the Emperor's poetic effusions were composed by the court poet. Here are some examples, all of which refer to Jehol.[1]

Written upon the return from hunting in Mulan:

I have returned from hunting in Mulan:
In the Summer Palace I rest from the saddle.
I have seen signs of a bountiful harvest
And I rejoice.
The springs on the hill-tops are for the deer to drink from.
The hills dress themselves in red leaves for man's delight.
Two years ago I let myself be persuaded to climb the hill;
Since then, I have seen the lonely pavilion on its top.

When, once again, I sit at this light window in the cloud-embowered pavilion,
I feel how swiftly time runs away, like water.
The mountains over the border are unequalled,
So is autumn in the Summer Palace gardens.
Junipers and pines clothe the hills with green:
Wild geese and ducks sport lazily on the blue river.
When I think of the past,
I am astonished that I have not been able to stifle all earthly cares.

---

[1] *Handbook of Jehol*, Part I, Chaps. 6, 7, 9. Translated by Mr. T. K. Koo.

Upon his return to the Summer Palace in 1753:

The Imperial banners float above the Summer Palace.
It is always in the clear autumn that I come.
The colours of the mountains never weary me.
The murmuring of the brooks is full of feeling.
Here and there stand maples, red among the green.
In place of cicadas, the crickets sing.
This year I have come too late to hunt;
I must set out again after some days' rest.

Upon arriving at Jehol, 1756:

I have visited every building on the hills and have explored the pine-decked valleys.
Water, stones, mountain mists and flowers make a fairy land.
Truly it is like a dwelling in the moon, far from the earth.
I delight in the joy of reading at the table by my study window.
Why does the deer cry out?
Why does the butterfly cast a shadow?
Last year's feasts were almost all for our distant vassals.
Anxious I sit, and wait for news of victory.

Upon the return to Jehol, after hunting, 1789:

I come to the Summer Palace three days after the hunt,
Gentle rain has washed away all dust and cooled the air.
It is very different from the deep mud last autumn.
I rejoice to see the green shoots of early grain.
Pines and firs appear in their green masses;
The wet brown leaves flutter along the ground
To hasten my departure,
For now it is time for the feast of Ch'ung Yang.[1]

---

[1] The Emperor always set out for the hunt a few days after the feast of mid-autumn and returned before the feast of Ch'ung Yang, which took place upon the 9th day of the 9th month.

Chapter IX

LORD MACARTNEY'S EMBASSY

Jehol, the Imperial City, is also associated with memories of the first embassy ever sent to an Emperor of China by an English King. Its head was Lord Macartney; its secretary, Sir George Staunton, who, in the absence of the Ambassador, had full powers as Minister Plenipotentiary. Staunton could speak the Chinese language. He has described the mission in an excellent work, *An Authentic Account of an Embassy from the King of Great Britain to the Emperor of China* (London, 1797).

On September 2nd, 1793, Lord Macartney, his suite and Chinese attendants, left Peking and travelled to the Imperial Summer Palace over the road I described in the first chapter. He himself rode in a European carriage which aroused the admiration of the officials after they had got over their first amazement at its swaying movement. They passed the pleasure pavilion where the Son of Heaven used to rest and, on the third day, reached a little town surrounded by a wall, and a river over which there was a bridge that was pulled down and replaced by a new one every time the Emperor crossed it. Among the hills they saw wild goats and wild horses.

On the fourth day the Great Wall came in sight. They were astonished that such a wall could have been erected along the tops of the hills and admired the power that lay behind such an achievement. It had been built two thousand years before as a protection against the Tartar hordes, but had lost its significance, as the Emperor now ruled over the lands on both sides of the wall. Through its gate they reached Koo-pei-koo (Ku-pei-k'ou), which had a strong garrison, where they were received with military honours. Their expert, Captain Parish, gives a detailed and accurate description of the Great Wall, and they remark on the peculiar fact that Marco Polo never mentioned that gigantic piece of architecture in his account of his travels.

Staunton says of the little Tartar dog: "It is a small species, with a long re-curved tail, of which caprice or fashion does not deprive him, and which is generally leaning to the left, as Linnaeus remarks of the domestic dog."

After travelling for seven days they reached Zhe-hol (Jehol), and discovered that, from the top of a hill in the palace park, the Emperor Ch'ien-lung was watching the brilliant procession and the military honours with which they were being received.

After the foreign guests had been shown to their quarters in the town, the prelude to the audience itself began. For the Englishman the chief aim of the whole journey was to open up trade facilities with China.[1]

For the Chinese, the important point was whether they would be able to make the foreigners fall to their knees and kotow (i.e. with their foreheads on the floor) to pay homage to the Son of Heaven. For no mortal had ever entered the presence of the Celestial Emperor without complying with the traditional directions for court ceremonial. These directions say, concerning audiences for the envoys of vassal princes :

> " When an audience had been requested, the officials of the residence for vassals' envoys shall instruct the envoy and his interpreters how they shall conduct themselves during the ceremony.
>
> " On the day of the audience the envoy, wearing the court dress of his country, and the interpreters wearing long jackets with breast-plates, are conducted to the palace gateway, and there they wait, humbly. The Emperor wears his ordinary dress and the court is held in the *Tien*,[2] where he usually rests. The Chamberlains of the Imperial Guard, the Assistant Chamberlains and the Imperial Body Guards, stand in rows on either side of the Emperor. Clad in the Dragon-robe with the long jacket with an embroidered

[1] Backhouse and Bland say concerning this : " For Englishmen, the reign of this great Emperor is particularly memorable in that it witnessed the first embassy from the King of Great Britain to the Court of China, that of the Earl of Macartney, in 1795, undertaken with the object of improving commercial relations between the Chinese authorities and the British merchants at Canton. Sir George Staunton's 'authentic account' of that embassy affords instructive reading to this day, besides giving a most interesting and sympathetic description of the aged monarch and his court at Jehol " (*Annals and Memoirs of the Court of Peking*, p. 311).

[2] Most of the vassals were received in the *ko* of the Purple Light, but envoys were not considered important enough to be received there. Lord Macartney was received in a tent.

breast-plate above it, the Minister of Rites leads the envoy and the interpreters to the west side of the *Tien* gateway where they perform the ceremony of the three kneelings and nine kotows. Then the envoy and one interpreter are led up the western steps and go to the door of Tien, where they fall on their knees. The Emperor asks a few questions, which are passed on by the Minister of Rites to the interpreter and translated by him for the envoy. The envoy's answer is interpreted for the Minister who repeats it to the Emperor. At the end of the audience, the envoy rises, and is conducted down the western steps and back to his residence." [1]

The Chinese wished the Englishmen to comply with the usual court ceremony for, in their opinion, George III was no more important than the Mongol vassal princes outside the Great Wall.

Already, in Tientsin, the question had been the subject of lively discussion among the officials, as we may see from "A letter from Chief Secretary Po Ho to Liang, the Governor of Chihli, for the information of Jui Tsêng, the Commissioner of the Salt Tax, written by order of the Emperor".[2] According to Mr. Koo it is plain to see from the letter what uneasiness was being caused at court and how cleverly they thought they had saved the Englishmen's faces by letting them come to the audience without leggings as these tight-fitting encumbrances would have prevented their kneeling and kotowing. The letter runs:

"The report (from the Governor and the Salt Commissioner) continues, that (the English) envoys at the banquet (in Tientsin) took off their hats and kotowed. But, accord-

[1] Translated by Mr. T. K. Koo from Ta Ch'ing Li T'ung, Chap. 45.
[2] *Historical Records*, Vol. 1, No. 5, translated by Mr. T. K. Koo.

ing to an earlier memorial concerning the meeting between Liang K'êng-tang and the envoys, they only took off their hats and stood respectfully when the Emperor's kind decree was made known to them. How then does it come about that this time the memorial says they took off their hats and kotowed?

"We have heard that Western people put leggings round their legs, which makes it uncomfortable for them to kneel and kotow. The memorial from the Governor and the Salt Commissioner has not made it clear whether they (the envoys) merely took off their hats and bowed, or kotowed properly. Therefore Jui Tsêng must be informed that, if the envoys at the banquet really kotowed, the matter may be allowed to drop, but if they merely removed their hats and bent their heads, then, when he talks to them, he must find an opportunity to tell them circumstantially that not only envoys of the vassal states have to perform the ceremony of the three kneelings and the nine kotows, but even their kings have to do the same when they are in audience with the Emperor. As their king has sent them to China to bring his good wishes, they must follow the Rites of the Celestial Court. As their habit of wearing leggings makes it impossible for them to kneel and kotow, they can remove them for the occasion, so that (they can) perform the ceremony and afterwards they can put them on again. This is very simple, and they ought not to hold too strictly to the customs of their own country. If they will not perform the ceremony, they will certainly not be carrying out their king's purpose in sending them so far across the sea to bring his congratulations and gifts. Moreover, they will cause the envoys of other states to laugh at them, and probably the court officials who are responsible for the Rites would not allow it. This must be conveyed as personal, friendly advice."

Upon the arrival of the Embassy in Jehol, this burning question had to be settled. Lord Macartney was too exalted to wait on the Prime Minister, whose title was Colao (Ko-lao) and who was styled Ho-choong-taung (Ho Shên).[1]

In his place he sent the Secretary of the Embassy, Staunton, who for the occasion bore the title of Minister Plenipotentiary.

The first questions asked by the Prime Minister, Ho Shên, concerned the reasons for the British Mission to China, and Staunton referred him to the King's letter which had been translated. Then there were long deliberations concerning the ceremonial kneeling, which the officials demanded. From the English point of view there should have been some differentiation between a great and independent king and the vassal princes of China. They had already remarked the fact that the king's gifts to the Emperor had been called 'tribute' by the Chinese, which intimated that they set the king on a level with their own vassals. The British answer was to the effect that there could not be any question of kneeling or kotowing.

During the conversations of the following days, the officials asked how far the Ambassador could go in showing reverence to the Emperor without overstepping his obligation to his own monarch.

The Earl answered that in the presence of his own King he bowed and knelt upon one knee, and that he was willing to show the same respect to the Emperor.

[1] According to Professor Lessing, Chung-t'ang was the title borne by members of the Privy Council.

The officials were to convey this information to the Court and let the Ambassador hear the Emperor's answer.

Presumably there was the same great anxiety in both camps. If the Emperor had felt inclined to insist upon the homage customary in China, the Earl would not have been able to comply, the whole Embassy would have been in vain, and the Englishmen would have had to go home with their errand unfulfilled. But the Emperor accepted the English point of view. Consequently, he doubtless considered that, for the first time in his life, he had graciously lowered himself to the level of his vassals, for among them he reckoned King George III of England, who had, of his own free will, sent special envoys with tribute. Staunton says: "This determination relieved the Ambassador from a load of much anxiety." This consideration or submission on the part of the Emperor was looked upon as something quite unheard-of. Because of it the Englishmen would certainly be still more hateful in the eyes of their Chinese and Tartar enemies, but, at the same time, their reputation would rise among the people.[1]

On the audience day, September 14th, the King's gifts were sent to the Palace and the Ambassador

[1] Backhouse and Bland add: "Ho Shên himself took a broad view of the Embassy's objects in coming to China, and remembering the friendly services rendered by the British at the end of the Nepalese Campaign, was instrumental in persuading the Emperor to waive the ceremony of the kotow, upon which the more conservative officials and courtiers were disposed to insist."

paid a visit to Ho Shên. They discussed trade relations, and the conversation was cordial and satisfactory. Ho Shên's utterances were clear and lucid and he gave the impression of being a clever statesman.

The Ambassador was ordered to be in the Palace Park before daybreak. A magnificent tent had been erected, supported by gilt and polished poles. Its interior had been tastefully and elegantly decorated, and on a platform stood the Emperor's throne, leading up to which there were flights of steps. In front of the audience tent were several smaller tents, one of which was placed at the disposal of the Embassy while they were waiting for the Emperor. In another were assembled the vassal princes from Tartary, Pegu, and other tributary states, who had come to offer their good wishes to the Emperor on his birthday. Others were for the Imperial princes and the officials. The place swarmed with important gentlemen wearing emblems of the Imperial Court, buttons, peacock feathers, and the golden dragon on a square field, on the fronts of their silk tunics. While waiting, the Emperor's brothers, sons, and grandsons visited the Ambassador in his tent.

Immediately after dawn there was a sound of music. The procession was approaching. Then came into sight the Imperial Guard, officers, members of the royal household, men with flags and umbrellas, and, in a palanquin carried by sixteen men, the Emperor Ch'ien-lung himself. He was dressed in simple dark silk, and wore a velvet cap like a Highlander's bonnet, ornamented in front with a big pearl. He mounted the throne. Ho Shên and two other officials kept close to him and addressed him always from their knees.

The President of the Tribunal of Rites led the Ambassador, his secretary, Staunton, a page, and an interpreter, to the left of the throne, which was the place of honour.

> "His Excellency was habited in a richly embroidered suit of velvet, adorned with the diamond badge and star of the Order of the Bath. Over this suit he wore a long mantle of the same order sufficiently ample to cover the limbs of the wearer. . . . The broad mantle which, as a Knight of the Order of the Bath, the Embassador was entitled to wear, was somewhat upon the plan of dress most pleasing to the Chinese. Upon the same principle, the Minister Plenipotentiary, being an Honorary Doctor of Laws at the University of Oxford, wore the scarlet gown of that degree." [1]

The outer garments were worn out of regard for the Asiatic dislike of showing the shape of the body, which was considered indecent.

At a sign, the Earl stepped forward to the throne and mounted the steps, bearing above his head "the large magnificent square box of gold, adorned with jewels". He went down on one knee and handed the casket containing the King's letter to the Emperor. Never before had a foreign envoy been allowed to mount the steps of the throne, and this exception

[1] *An authentic account of an Embassy from the King of Great Britain to the Emperor of China* (London, 1797), Vol. 2, pp. 230–1.

produced a great impression on everyone. Court gossip asserted afterwards that the noble Lord had been so overcome in the presence of the mighty ruler that his legs gave way and he fell upon all fours. If he had refused to kotow of his own accord, the presence of the Emperor had obliged him to do so.

The Emperor received the letter with his own hands and expressed the "satisfaction that he felt at the testimony which His Britannic Majesty gave to him of his esteem and goodwill in sending him an Embassy, with a letter, and rare presents, that he, on his part, entertained sentiments of the same kind towards the Sovereign of Great Britain and hoped that harmony should always be maintained among their respective subjects."[1]

The Emperor then handed the Earl a sceptre of jade, the symbol of fortune and peace. After some conversation the Earl presented his own gifts to the Emperor and received gifts in return.

The artist of the mission made a sketch of the Emperor, of which Staunton says that it is not at all like him, for the Emperor's eyes were more full and clear and his expression more open and friendly. It is reproduced in the first volume of Staunton's book, and has little likeness to the contemporary Chinese portraits, one of which is reproduced here (Pl. XXXVI).

The Englishmen were invited to sit on cushions to the left of the throne while the envoys from Pegu and the districts near the Caspian Sea were received.

[1] Op. cit., Vol. 2, p. 234.

These had to kotow nine times, and were hastily dismissed. Finally small tables were set out and a banquet served. Staunton says:

"The commanding feature of the scene was the calm dignity and the sober pomp of Asiatic grandeur which European refinements have not yet attained."

The Emperor honoured his guests by himself handing them the drinking-cups and he expressed his hope that the king would attain to the same advanced age as his own; he was 83 years old and in full possession of his health and strength.

Finally Ch'ien-lung stepped down from the throne and walked, with upright carriage and firm step, to the palanquin.

On a later day the Emperor gave orders that the guests should be taken round the palace park, and they had as guide Ho Shên, the Prime Minister himself, "he whom people looked upon as almost a second Emperor." They rode round among the fairy-like beauty of the groves of trees among the hills of Jehol, and admired the seventy-two pavilions, temples, and other 'beautiful places' which the Emperor and his famous grandfather had built, in whose various halls they saw many objects of art from Europe. They went on the lake in graceful boats, and everywhere they saw deer, harts and rare birds, while the ponds were full of beautiful gold fish. Ho Shên was courteous and affable.

In a certain part of the park there was a boundary beyond which no human being might pass except the

Emperor and the eunuchs. There, hidden in the secret groves, were the palaces of the Empresses, princesses, concubines and slaves. In all probability it was there that the famous Turkish beauty, the Princess Hsiang Fei, was established for at least one summer. We shall tell of her tragic fate in a later chapter.

On the Emperor's birthday, September 17th, the Ambassador received an invitation to a review at which Captain Parish estimated 12,000 officers and 80,000 troops were present.

For several days there were feasts, entertainments, music, dancing, acting, and fireworks. The Emperor summoned Lord Macartney and explained that it was only upon such occasions as this that he amused himself; at other times he devoted himself to the cares of his kingdom and subjects. He sent the English king one of his poems as a sign of friendship, and some gems that had been in his family for eight hundred years.

On September 21st the English Embassy returned to Peking. Their mission had been fulfilled and they could return home.

What did the Chinese really think of that stately and splendid embassy, with the wealth that it displayed, of the royal gifts, the large suite, their ship, and all that they brought with them?[1] To outward appearance they were courteous and condescending,

[1] The cost of the gifts, £13,123 12*s*. 4*d*., was defrayed by The East India Company.—(Translator's note.)

but within they were scornful and supercilious. The Manchu Dynasty was at its zenith. In Peking and Jehol, men were accustomed to seeing princes and envoys from all the lands of Asia competing with one another in humiliating themselves before the Son of Heaven. Now came tribute-bearers from across the far western sea, from an unknown vassal who at least was loyal, and trembled before the might of the Emperor. S. Wells Williams says of this embassy, that the Chinese "probably dismissed it with the feeling that it was one of the most splendid testimonials of respect that a tributary nation had ever paid their court. The English were henceforth registered among the nations who had sent their tribute-bearers and were consequently only the more bound to obey the injunctions of their master."[1]

In English Oriental politics Macartney's Embassy was an event of the greatest importance. Witness the immense cost, the imposing numbers of its personnel, the ship, the trappings, the gifts, and everything else. By the Chinese the whole thing was belittled as an almost comic episode, scarcely worth including in the records. In the chronicles of Ch'ien-lung's 58th year, the English Embassy is mentioned with the greatest casualness.[2]

"(In the 5th month the Emperor left, etc.) The 3rd day of the 7th month (August 9th) the Emperor, at shooting practice, inspected the Manchu troops stationed at Jehol.

[1] *The Middle Kingdom*, Vol. II, p. 454.
[2] *Handbook of Jehol*, Part I, chap. 20.

. . . The 27th day (Sept. 2nd) the Emperor received in audience in Ch'uan-a-shêng-ching the envoys from Burma, for whom he gave a dinner . . . The 10th day of the 8th month (Sept. 14th) the Emperor received the English Chief Ambassador, and his associate envoy, Staunton, in the Garden of Ten Thousand Trees. For them, princes and envoys from Burma, and several others, the Emperor gave a banquet. The 13th day (Sept. 17th), which was his birthday, the Emperor received congratulations from the princes and from the Burmese and English envoys. The Emperor went to Ch'uan-a-shêng-ching, where he gave a dinner for them. This was repeated on the two following days. The 20th (Sept. 24th) the Emperor left Jehol."

The English ambassadors were placed on the same level as the Mongol princes and the envoys from Burma.

What the Emperor, the Son of Heaven, thought of England and its king, he showed plainly enough in the answer he gave to King George III. It is reproduced in the third part of Chang-ku-ts'ung-pien, or the *Collection of Material for the Study of History*, published by the historical section of the Palace Museum in 1928, which Professor Lessing has kindly translated for me. The document is not called a 'letter' but a 'decree or edict' "drawn up on the 29th day of the 6th month (of the 58th year of Ch'ien-lung), delivered the 19th day of the 8th month."

"We, who have been invested by Heaven with the responsibility for the fate of Our Empire, inform and notify the King of England.[1]

[1] The expression 'king' was only used of tribute-paying vassals. To 'inform' and 'notify' has an underlying contemptuous meaning implying a peremptory order.

"You, O King, who dwell far across remote oceans, have manifested your appreciation of our culture by sending special envoys with a humbly formulated petition. These have sailed over the seas and have come to our Court to kotow, wish us good-fortune on our birthday, and, at the same time, to bring us the products of your country, thereby showing the sincerity of your friendliness. We have read your honestly and sincerely worded application and have from it, O King, seen the genuineness of your feelings, and your submissive devotion, and we have graciously taken cognizance of it.

"In consideration of the fact that the first and second envoys brought the petition and tribute in accordance with their mission and made the long journey here, we will give them proof of our favour and friendliness and have commanded our minister to bring them to an audience. We have deigned to arrange a banquet for them and have rewarded them far more than is usual. Although they alone came to Peking, the ship's officers and men, to the number of over six hundred, who have returned to Chushan, have been rewarded by us, so that our favours might embrace all, as we have the same love for all.[1]

"You request in your petition our permission to send a person from your land to live at the Celestial Court and superintend the trade interests of your country. Certainly we have, heretofore, permitted strangers from the western ocean who evinced a wish to come to the Celestial Court and to take up an official position there, to do so, but only on condition that they obediently wore the dress and colours of the Celestial Court, allowed themselves to be housed in halls (detached houses) and undertook never to return home. Even you, O King, should know that this is an unalterable rule of the Celestial Court.

"Now you ask, O King, that you may be permitted to send a person from your land to live in the Capital. But

[1] 'All' meaning Chinese and Barbarians. The Englishmen belonged to the latter.

as, unlike other people from the western ocean in our Capital, he cannot always stay in Peking without ever returning home, and as we cannot allow him to travel here and there to carry intelligence, it would be of no value. Moreover, the lands which are ruled by the Celestial Court are vast and far-reaching. For the envoys of the border tribes there are hard and fast rules concerning their translation duties, maintenance, deportment and all their movements, and it would be impossible to allow them to move about freely.[1] Now, if your land sends someone to Peking, he will not understand the language; the manner of dressing and decoration are different, and there is no place where he can live. If he says he is ordered to dress in the same manner as the rest of the people from the western ocean who are in Peking, the Celestial Court has never before cared to bring force to bear in this direction. If, for example, the Celestial Court wished to have a perpetual envoy in your land, how would your land meekly put up with it? Then, too, there are a great number of western lands; your land is not the only one concerned. If all, like you, O King, asked to be allowed to send men to dwell in Peking, how could it be allowed in every case? In no circumstances could such a thing be considered even for a moment. How could we, at your request, disregard the venerable laws and rules of the Celestial Court?

"When it is said that you, O King, out of solicitude for your trade wish to send us an envoy, it must be observed that for some time people from your country have been trading in Macao, and have always been graciously tolerated by us. Even before, when Portugal and Italy repeatedly sent envoys to our Court, with petitions for trade protection, the Celestial Court, realizing the uprightness and sincerity of their prayers, granted them special privileges and allowed full facilities for their trade.

"When the merchant Wu Chao-p'ing of Canton was in debt to a foreign ship, the Governor-General of the Province

[1] Here Englishmen are included in the border tribes.

was ordered to pay what was due out of the money from the provincial taxes, and the negligent debtor was severely punished, which is a thing that should be known in your country.

"Why do foreigners crave the unprecedented privilege of sending someone to Peking? Such a one would find himself at a distance of 10,000 *li* from the trading centre, Macao. How then could he watch over trade interests?

"When it is said that people look with wondering admiration at the Celestial Court and wish to study and follow its culture, it should be remembered that the Celestial Court has rules and laws of its own which are very different from those in your country.

"The person you, O King, would send here might be familiar with the customs, laws, and ceremonials of your own country, but he could never imitate (those of) China, and, if he could, no useful purpose would be served.

"The Celestial Court rules (the people) within the four seas. Its first object is to keep the land in order, and to direct the administration. For it rarity and costliness have no value; but in consideration (of the fact) that with an honest motive you brought us those objects from afar we have ordered the proper authorities to receive them.[1] In reality the influence of the Celestial Court is far-reaching, and princes from ten thousand lands come to our audiences. Every possible object of value comes across the mountains and even the sea, and everything imaginable is collected here, as the first and second envoys have seen. Therefore rare and valuable objects are not appreciated, and we have not the slightest need of the products of your land, O King.

"As your desire to send a person to reside in Peking is contrary to the order and regulation of the Celestial Court, and as it could scarcely be of the least advantage to your country, we are sending the tribute-bearers with these

[1] A discourteous expression; approximately—to record, or register them.

careful instructions, on a safe road home. You, O King, must understand our wishes and continue to strive to be faithful and upright, and swear eternal devotion and obedience, and so protect and order your land that together (with us) you may enjoy peace.

"In that we gave to the first and second envoys, together with their staff, interpreters, and soldiers, the usual rewards, even some few extra rewards, which are entered upon a separate list, we take the opportunity of your envoys returning to your land to announce our wish, and we send you, O King, with graciousness in addition to the usual rarities and valuables, all manner of patterned silks and costly writing materials, which are noted down on a separate list.

"Receive them humbly and bear in mind our Imperial wishes.

"This is our All Highest decree."

In Ch'ien-lung's 58th year, in the 8th month and on the day Chi-mou, the Emperor sent to the King of England a second 'instruction' which contains a great many points not included in the first one.[1]

1. The request of the English for the opening of general trade was refused with the intimation that China herself produced all she required. Trade in porcelain, silk, and tea was allowed on the same terms as before. Any alteration in trade conditions with foreigners was disallowed.

2. The request for new trading stations in Ning-po, on the Chu-shan islands, in Tientsin, and Canton was refused, as hitherto all strangers had traded in Macao (*sic* !). "A permission that the barbarians of your

[1] It is given in full by Backhouse and Bland. I quote here a summary from Professor F. Lessing's translation of the original documents.

land have hitherto agreed to." In the places mentioned, there had been neither Hong-merchants (trading firms), interpreters, nor trade facilities.

3. The request for a warehouse in Peking was refused, because such a thing would be incompatible with conditions in China. This did not refer to the Russians, as the latter had enjoyed privileges only so long as Kiakhta was not open. Peking was much farther away from England than Canton and nearer to Russia.

4. A request for an anchorage near the Chu-shan islands was refused for the same reason. It was pointed out that even the smallest piece of Chinese soil was under rigid discipline, and that the Emperor could not create a precedent.

5. The request for a trade emporium for the English barbarian merchants in Canton was dismissed, as Macao was sufficient for everyone. Hong-merchants had been appointed there to act as go-betweens between the foreigners and the Chinese, to avoid friction. Even here the Emperor must avoid creating a precedent, and for that reason no freedom of movement was allowed.

6. The request for the abolition of, or at least a decrease in, the dues for English ships that trafficked on the Pearl River between Macao and Canton was refused. Reference was made to the great number of ships, and it was pointed out that the same dues must be paid by all.

7. A request for uniform charges in all the harbours

of China was dismissed, because only the harbour of Canton came into the matter.

8. A request for freedom for religious propaganda was refused, with a reference to the ancient Chinese doctrines which formed the foundations of the Chinese State.

The Emperor maintained that these demands rested upon the King of England's deficient understanding of the Chinese Empire, or upon the arbitrariness of his servants. Because of the great distance of England from China, the Emperor had made the rewards sent to the King of England bigger than usual. The Emperor reckoned upon this being understood, and expected humble obedience.

This final claim has been translated by Backhouse and Bland as follows:

> "It may be, O King, that the above proposals have been wantonly made by your Ambassador on his own responsibility, or peradventure you yourself are ignorant of our dynastic regulations, and had no intention of transgressing them when you expressed these wild ideas and hopes. I have ever shown the greatest condescension to the tribute missions of all States which sincerely yearn after the blessings of civilization so as to manifest my kindly indulgence. I have even gone out of my way to grant any requests which were in any way consistent with Chinese usage. Above all, upon you, who live in a remote and inaccessible region far across the spaces of ocean, but who have shown your submissive loyalty by sending this tribute mission, I have heaped benefits far in excess of those accorded to other nations. But the demands presented by your embassy are not only a contravention of dynastic tradition but would be utterly unproductive of good result to yourself, besides

being quite impracticable. I have accordingly stated the facts to you in detail, and it is your bounden duty reverently to appreciate my feelings, and to obey these instructions henceforward for all time, so that you may enjoy the blessings of perpetual peace. If, after the receipt of this explicit decree, you lightly give ear to the representations of your subordinates, and allow your barbarian merchants to proceed to Chêkiang or Tientsin with the object of landing and trading there, the ordinances of my Celestial Empire are strict in the extreme, and the local officials, both civil and military, are bound reverently to obey the law of the land. Should your vessels touch the shore, your merchants will assuredly never be permitted to land or to reside there, but will be subject to instant expulsion. In that event your barbarian merchants will have had a long journey for nothing. Do not say that you were not warned in due time! Tremblingly obey, and show no negligence. A special mandate."[1]

Any comment on this haughty and contemptuous reply to the King of England is unnecessary, but it is interesting to compare the manner in which Ch'ien-lung received the King's envoy with the deference and obsequiousness with which, thirteen years earlier, he had received the Tashi Lama. For him the King of England was merely one vassal among hundreds, whereas the Tashi Lama had power over all the Lamaist lands which were under the rule of the Middle Kingdom. In the opinion of the Emperor, Tibet was of far greater importance than Great Britain.

But if this answer, given during the last period of China's greatness, was an affront to the majesty of

[1] Backhouse and Bland, *Annals and Memoirs of the Court of Peking*, p. 330.

England, the latter took royal and barbarous revenge during the following century.

In the ' tribute lists ' of the English Embassy, which have been translated for me by Professor Lessing, the following articles are mentioned :

1. An astronomical instrument, called, in the language of the western land, a planetarium, showing the sun, moon and stars, and a detailed globe of the earth. On the planetarium, in accordance with its dimensions, the earth is quite small. All the units are movable according to their natural courses: eclipses of the sun and moon, and the culminations of the stars can be demonstrated on the apparatus, as well as years, seasons, months, days, and hours. This is a new and useful apparatus, a unique and wonderful contrivance that has been thought out and worked upon for years by a famous astronomer. It took 15 cases to hold the gigantic instrument, and the embassy has brought special mechanics to set it up, men who assisted in its construction. They request that His Majesty will allow them enough time to set it up. With it there is a *lai-fu-lai-ko'tu-erh* (refractor) for the observation of the smallest and most distant stars in the plainest movement.

A newly discovered instrument by the astronomer, Hê-chih-êrh (? Herschel).[1]

2. A clock resembling an astronomical instrument by which one can easily explain and reconcile the

[1] According to the East India Company's Factory Records, this instrument was made by Herschel.—(Translator's note.)

movements of the sun, moon, and stars in the heavens. It is useful in the study of astronomy and geography. It is packed in three light and easily transportable cases. The mechanics came with the mission to Peking.

3. A perfect celestial globe, painted in blue to resemble the sky, with the stars in gold and silver of different sizes and colours (*sic*) so that it is as if one were looking at the heavens ; and it has a " measuring-net " of silver thread.[1]

4. A terrestrial globe, upon which are shown all the Lord's countries, the four continents, mountains, rivers, and islands, also the sea-routes and ships of the ' red woolly ones '.[2]

5. Eleven boxes containing various instruments for determination of time, the phases of the moon, and the forecasting of the weather, all made by clever craftsmen.

6. A meteorological apparatus very useful for making weather observations.

7. An exercising apparatus for increasing muscular strength.

8. An ingeniously devised chair that, if one so desires, can be set in motion when one is sitting on it.

9. A chest containing ancient and modern examples of flagons and boxes,[3] also a tinder box that can

[1] Measuring-net—Movable meridians ; two sliding circles and pieces, two quadrants of altitude, two horary wires and four centre pieces (Factory Records).—(Translator's note.)

[2] By the ' red woolly ones ' was meant the English.

[3] " Specimens of the modes in which the Best British Artists work and improve the clayey and stoney substances of their own country " (Factory Records).—(Translator's note.)

melt glass and china, consisting of a burning mirror (lens) made by a famous craftsman out of an enormous piece of glass which, if held against the sun, will not only burn plants and wood but even melt gold, silver, copper, iron, and platinum. If there were no fire on earth one could burn and melt with this mirror. It is of enormous strength.

10. Various engravings, among them a family group of the 'red woolly' English King, pictures of towns, fortifications, long bridges, buildings, gardens, villages, battles, and marvellous foreign ships.

11. Two lamps, with inlaid glass, for lighting a palace apartment.

12. Some fine, gold-woven mats for use in a house.[1]

13. Some big carpets for covering the floors in the palace.

14. A pair of fine, beautifully made yellow saddles —the very best work, humbly offered to His Majesty the Emperor for his personal use.

15. Two carriages, one for warm and one for cold weather, humbly offered to His Majesty the Emperor for his own use.

16. Various weapons, for the use of His Majesty the Emperor, including long and short self-lighting fire-arms,[2] knives and swords which can cut through copper and iron.

[1] Various pieces of tapestry and hangings for the Imperial apartments made of satin and woollen cloth painted or varnished with gold (Factory Records).—(Translator's note.)

[2] Muskets and pistols, and one pair of Magazine Pistols, that fire eight times at one loading (Factory Records).—(Translator's note.)

17. Some bronze cannon and melon cannon (? mortars) for use in training troops, and a small detachment of soldiers from the 'land of the red woollies', who arrived at Peking with the envoys. If His Majesty wishes to see the way in which European cannon are used, they can show him.

18. Models in gold and silver of the big and small warships of the 'red woollies'. In spite of their difference in size, they are all faithful models of the originals. On the big warships are a hundred great cannon, of which one can get a good idea from these models. The land of the 'red woolly ones' is the greatest land among those in the western sea. They possess several great ships. They wished to send the tribute-bearing envoys to the Celestial Court on the largest one, but the water outside the harbour was too shallow, so that they could not have entered the harbour. So they sent the middle-sized ones and small ones, that they could land and reach Peking. As an expression of their sincerity and the depth of their affection, they have brought a model of a great warship as a tribute to His Majesty.

19. Various products of the land of the 'red-woollies' wrapped in packets, also all kinds of handiwork, weavings, blankets, fine cotton goods, steel and iron articles, as tribute to His Majesty.

During the misfortunes that overtook Peking and its Palaces in later days, it is probable that these truly regal presents were either lost or confiscated and taken back to Europe.

CHAPTER X

HSIANG FEI, THE CONCUBINE OF AN EMPEROR

IN the south part of Peking's Chinese city, surrounded by fields and simple huts, there stands a temple, where the cultured sages and poets of the Manchu period used to meet to enjoy the delights of the country and amuse themselves with intellectual conversation. The place was called T'ao-jan-ting, or The Summer-House of Delight.

The present day, with its dry, prosaic outlook on life, has no need of summer-houses, and for twenty years no joyous gathering has met at T'ao-jan-ting. The temple halls are ruined and deserted. Two poverty-stricken serving brothers still keep watch over that relic of a greater and richer time.

Near the temple, on one side of a hill, stands a gravestone, two feet high (Pl. XLV). A weeping willow casts its shadow over it. On the front of the stone is the inscription—" The Grave of the Sweet Scented One ", and on the other side this verse :

" O deep sorrow, O lamentation without end.
The short song has died away,
And the moon's light paled.

Dark shadows sink over the land
Where to a precious stone your blood is turned,
But even the precious stone must change.
The sweet odour alone remains for ever.
Tell me, is it the truth, or only a dream.
A butterfly emerging from its chrysalis ?" [1]

In olden times this was the burial-place of the hetairæ, and here was buried a lady of pleasure who had the same marvellous attributes and the same name as the Emperor Ch'ien-lung's favourite concubine, the Princess Hsiang Fei from Aksu in Eastern Turkistan. A poor youth and this girl had sworn that they would love one another for ever, and when she was sold to a rich merchant she took her life in order not to break the oath she had sworn to her beloved. He buried her under this simple monument and on the back of it carved the poem in which he gave expression to his grief.

Misled by the similarity in the names, unknown writers seized upon the romantic gravestone and connected it with the mysterious figure of the Emperor's favourite. The simple verse was ascribed to the court poet, and the dreamers and roysterers who entertained one another at T'ao-jan-ting could smilingly assert that here was the place of peace where rested that tender creature, who, more than any other human being, had possessed the love of the mighty Emperor.

[1] Professor Lessing informs me that this verse is taken word for word from a poem written by the famous Emperor Wu of the Han Dynasty, which was inspired by the conjuring up of his dead concubine, the renowned Li Fu-jên, by the Taoist, Shao Wêng, in 121 B.C.

Beside it is another tombstone with a short but enlightening inscription: "The resting-place of drunken Kuo." Perhaps he was the boon companion who, inspired by the perfume which still hovered about the spot, engraved the verse in honour of Hsiang Fei.

Eastern Turkistan had been a Turkish vassal state under the Eleut since the Eleut King, Galdan, established the Mohammedan dynasty of Hodja in Yarkand in 1678. In 1757 the land was ruled by two brothers, Burhan-al-Din and Khozi Khan, generally called the big and the little Hodjas. About that time the two brothers seized the opportunity of trouble between the Eleut and the Chinese, to fight among themselves. When the Chinese had beaten the Eleut, they turned their attention to the Hodjas. In 1758 General Chao Huei marched from Ili to Tarim. The two princes defended themselves bravely, the elder in Kashgar, the younger in Yarkand, but in 1759 both towns fell, and the Hodjas fled to Badakshan. The prince of that place beheaded them and sent the heads to Peking. Eastern Turkistan was then named Kansu-Sin-kiang.

After having described the fate of Amursana and the skilful return march of General Chao Huei eastwards from the Ili valley, Professor Karlgren describes these events as follows:

"The time had arrived for the Emperor to deal firmly with the situation, and through the agency of General Chao Huei, who was given a free hand and sufficient troops, there was a thorough and decisive reconstruction of the whole of Central Asia. The Eleuts were defeated in 1757 and the last remaining hordes fled into Russian territory, or were deported by the Chinese to the northern boundary of Kansu. Dzungaria and Ili were depopulated and the room thus made was filled up with Chinese in the usual manner.

"Chao Huei's victorious march reached as far as the Eleut's vassals, the Mohammedan princes in Kashgar. After comprehensive operations and severe fighting, Tashkent and Kashgar were taken, and the last princes of Kashgar fled to the Mohammedan Sultan of Badakshan. The latter, terrified to find a Chinese army threatening his borders, killed them and sent their heads to Peking (1759). The inhabitants of the Tarim lands, who, for the most part, were Islamic descendants of the older Turkish races, were now removed by the Chinese to Ili and Dzungaria; thus Central Asia became definitely Islamized."[1]

Grousset says:

"The conquest of Ili and Kashgar by Ch'ien-lung finally completed the programme that the Chinese policy in Central Asia had been striving for during eighteen centuries. So great was the prestige gained by China that the Torgot, who had emigrated to the Volga in Russia, returned in 1771 to settle down in Chinese Turkistan."[2]

The following story of a woman, romanticized in places, has an historical background. Hsiang Fei was the consort of Khozi Khan, 'the little Hodja'.

It was in the twenty-fourth year of the Emperor's reign that his armies, under the command of the victorious general, Chao Huei, made war on Eastern Turkistan.

[1] Norstedt's *Världshistoria*, Vol. XV, p. 258.
[2] *Histoire de l'Extrême Orient*, Vol. II, pp. 539–40.

From the Emperor's all-powerful favourite, Ho Shên, the man who had received Lord Macartney, the general had received orders to keep an eye open for the younger Hodja's consort, the Princess Hsiang Fei, 'The Perfumed One'. The Emperor, who had heard of her marvellous beauty and the intoxicating perfume that emanated from her, was interested to know what had happened to her.

After the end of the campaign, Chao Huei received orders from the Emperor, brought by special couriers, to return to Peking with his armies.

During his campaign Chao Huei had not forgotten the orders he had received from Ho Shên, and this is where the Chinese story begins.

Where was the lovely princess to be found? Probably in the district where her husband had been killed. She might be in Badakshan. The general demanded her surrender. It appeared that not the least important reason for the killing of the younger Hodja by the Sultan of Badakshan was the latter's desire to seize the young man's wife. She was famous throughout Central Asia. But he was disappointed; nothing he could do brought him nearer to the attainment of his desires. He threatened her. She called him a murderer who had killed her husband. She would sooner die than belong to him.

Then came General Chao Huei's demand for her surrender. The Sultan answered: "Hsiang Fei is the most lovely of all Mohammedan women. To win her is not easy. To give up that perfumed flower is still harder. I will exchange her for ten pairs of rings of white jade from Honan."

Chao Huei agreed.

Clad in his robes of office, the general received her in his tent. He found her sunken in despair and learned that she would neither eat nor drink. If she had succeeded in taking her life, the Emperor's anger would have fallen upon him, so he resorted to subterfuge. He assured her that her husband was held a prisoner in Badakshan, that China was demanding his surrender, and that he was to be taken to Peking, where he would be pardoned and sent back to Aksu with his wife. He sent for her chief ladies-in-waiting and bribed them to calm her. They were commanded to see that her food was prepared by orthodox Mohammedans, and to carry out all her wishes. In order that the long journey from Aksu to Peking should not tire her, the wheels of her carriage were wrapped in strips of felt, and the windows hung with brocade. The carriage was so large that she could lie down in it. In addition to her two favourite ladies, she had twenty slave girls and as many servants, and she always had her own guard of soldiers. As she was accustomed to a daily bath of sheep's milk and koumis, it was arranged that these luxuries should be provided on the journey. After her bath her women rubbed her with perfume and she rinsed her mouth with scented tea. In this way she kept her skin soft and white, and an intoxicating perfume followed her wherever she went. Not only men, but women, were bewitched by her beauty and charm. Everyone showed her the greatest respect. It was known that the Emperor was awaiting her in Peking.

With the armies was the eighteen-year-old Fu K'ang-an, who was believed to be the natural son of the Emperor, and afterwards became famous because of his brilliant campaign against the Gurkhas in Nepal (1792). They often talked together, and she jested with him and teased him. She appeared to have forgotten her sorrow, but probably she was only upheld by the hope of seeing her husband again.

The journey took six months. For the most part they followed the road that Marco Polo had taken five hundred years before ; and at the Lu-kou-ch'ao bridge, which is called the Marco Polo bridge, and is mentioned by the great Venetian in his travels, the victorious army and its general were received with signal honours.

The Emperor was anxiously waiting to see the Princess from Aksu. Their first meeting took place one evening in a room of the old Summer Palace which had been built by the Jesuits. The Emperor had ordered the eunuchs to lead the princess to his private apartment. Before she entered the room he was conscious of an intoxicating perfume of lotus blooms, but it was neither the scent of flowers nor perfume ; it was something superhuman which surrounded her with a mysterious atmosphere.

She stepped proudly and defiantly into the presence of the autocrat. It was this man who by his wars had brought about her husband's death. At the same time she could not overcome her shyness. She refused to greet him. She did not deign to favour him with a single glance, but wept silently.

He, the Son of Heaven, the ruler of the whole world, who was revered and worshipped as a god by hundreds of millions, was powerless before the Princess from Aksu.

She was no figure of fiction, this young queen from Eastern Turkistan, she was a real historical personality. Had she given way to the Emperor's desire, she would have been able to play an influential part, like Yang Kuei-fei at the court of the Emperor Ming during the T'ang Dynasty. But she remained steadfast. Her virtue and constancy could not be shaken by the greatest man of the age. Her memory still lives among the people of China. Her portrait, painted by the Jesuit Father Castiglione, is preserved in the Palace Museum (Pl. XLVI) and, in 1928, her picture was still printed on the notes of the China and South Sea Bank. Modern plays and romances have been written about her, from which, at my request, Professor Lessing has taken the material that has been used for the following sketch of her relations with the Emperor Ch'ien-lung.

Now she stood before the Emperor. He was overwhelmed at the first glance, and could only gaze and gaze. This was no woman, but a being from another world. He tried to master himself and stared at her fixedly. She blushed slightly. Her eyebrows arched above her eyes. Her eyelashes were long. Her lips shone cherry-red and her teeth snow-white. Her hair fell raven black upon her white shoulders. She was slender and well grown, and her hands seemed half transparent, like pale crystals.

The Emperor sat lost in thought, admiring her. He saw her surrounded by a shimmer of celestial purity and perfection, and shining with an outer and inner beauty that was unearthly. Every sensuous thought vanished. Never had he seen anything so wonderful in human guise. He dared not touch her finger-tips. He sat there, as if in a dream, sighed and whispered: "Oh, what beauty! What a heavenly vision! You alone possess the holiest breath of heaven and earth. Why have I never before had the felicity of seeing you? What can I do to please you?"

At last he returned to reality, respectfully presented her with a bracelet of pearls and a sceptre of jade, the symbol of good fortune, which she received without a word of thanks, and then he gave the sign that she was to be conducted back to her own apartments.

To her ladies who were present, he said: "It is not to be wondered at that she is shy and lost, here in this strict ceremonial of our court, and with a burden of sorrow and longing in her heart. Has she not left her home ten thousand *li* from here? Comfort her; fulfil her every desire and convey her wishes to the chief-eunuch. He who neglects his duties towards her shall be executed; he who wins her affection shall be rewarded."

When Hsiang Fei was back in her apartment, she began to laugh and jest and play with her ladies. They whispered together: "How strange! Before the Emperor she was like an image, ice-cold, hard and stiff, and never even thanked him for his gifts. Now she is gay and plays with us like a child."

Her palace stood in a wonderful garden and there she spent her days. She rowed with her ladies upon the lakes, climbed up the hill on the Island of Jasper, fished in the waters, or hunted roe-deer in the park. There one could often hear the cry: "His Majesty waits upon Hsiang Fei!" Her ladies tried to persuade her to meet the Emperor, but she fled up Chai-tsing-lou, the "Tower from which the Stars are Plucked", and a eunuch had to carry word to the Emperor that she could not be found.

One day the Emperor went to Hsiang Fei's room. When still some distance away he heard her merry laughter; he stopped outside the door and peeped round the edge of the hangings. She was sitting with her hair outspread and her bosom bare, being waited upon by a couple of ladies-in-waiting, while two palace girls lay on the floor, their breasts serving her for a footstool. In front of her were two bowls full of pearls, the gift of the Emperor. She gave some to the two ladies, and the remainder she threw about the room by the handful, and the serving girls fell upon them. When the Emperor had seen enough he stepped into the room, laughing. All the women fell on their faces ; only Hsiang Fei sat still and seemed not to notice him. She dressed her hair in front of the mirror. The Emperor sat down opposite her, but she never even glanced at him. At last he withdrew, troubled and gloomy.

He took counsel of his favourite, Ho Shên, and wondered if the people would consider it too great a kindness if, instead of putting to death the consort of the rebellious prince, he shut her up in his women's quarters. Ho Shên pointed out that it was customary to treat women taken prisoner in war in such a manner. He advised the Emperor to have built within the palace a little Mohammedan town, with bazaars, gardens, and mosques, just like her own Aksu. Chao Huei had been there, and he could make the plans. Her court ought to be Mohammedan, as was her kitchen.

The Emperor followed his advice. In the Jesuits' palace he had a tower erected by builders from Khotan. On its top was an enormous mirror like a moon, and in its interior were set up crystals that shone like stars. There, a hundred Chinese girls sang and danced the rainbow dance, a hundred Mohammedan girls sang sad songs from Kucha, and a hundred girls from Europe clashed cymbals, till they rang like spears and clanged like swords.

She was led into all this beauty that was to remind her of her home. She looked about and wept. But the story goes that she often sat in the tower and looked at the mosque, where a holy mullah recited the prayers of the Prophet and her far-away home—' La illaha il Allah.'[1]

The Emperor often complained about the state of affairs to the chief eunuch, Ch'ui. That she was elevated to the rank of Kuei-jên or concubine of the 4th class pleased her least of all, but it improved her position at court. Nor were her sorrow and homesickness diminished by the costly works of art she was given; a tree of coral a foot high with a trunk as thick as a man's arm, a chalk-white jade vase two feet high, decorated with beautifully carved human figures, a melon of green jade with a stalk and leaves upon which sat a grasshopper with a blue head and green wings, and flowers and bowls of jade and carnelian, cups of rock crystal, a bath of pure gold, and countless other precious things. She cared for none of them; she scarcely noticed them.

The Emperor had a palace built for her in Nan-hai, where she could be more undisturbed. There too was a tower, Wang-chia-lou (the tower from which one can see one's own country).

One day the Emperor, intoxicated, and supported by a eunuch, went to Hsiang Fei's apartment. Her ladies urged her to rise and greet him, but she remained

[1] The mosque Ch'ien-lung built for the comfort of Hsiang Fei is no myth, but a reality. In 1912 it was still standing, although in a ruined condition, outside the south wall of the Lake Palace of the Forbidden City. Until the year 1908 an old Dungana Mullah, who was a Hadji (having made the pilgrimage to Mecca), held services in the mosque. In May 1912, the President, Yuan Shih-k'ai, had the ruined temple pulled down, and with it vanished the last monument of Hsiang Fei's moving love story, and her tragic fate in Peking.

sitting, her eyes downcast and mutinous. " Is the lovely one embarrassed ? " shouted the Emperor, laughing, and he motioned to the others to go away. When he was alone with her, he sat down at her side, took her by the wrist and whispered amorously ; " What a soft, white arm ! "

Swift as lightning she drew a dagger and would have stabbed him, if he had not had the presence of mind to parry the blow. The point of the dagger grazed his arm and he bled profusely. He was sober in an instant, and staunched the flow of blood with his ample sleeve, but wide red stains spread over the golden dragons on his tunic. He let her ladies bind up his wound, and went out, while Hsiang Fei cried that she wished to return home.

The next day she went with her attendants to the 'Tower from which one can see one's own country', but the sight of the mosque and the Mohammedans only served to increase her longing.

Still she was touched by the Emperor's compassion and his kindness about the Mohammedans, and, one day, she acceded to his repeated prayers that she should dance the sword dance of her country. She threw off her fur robe and took up her position in front of the Emperor ; slowly and graciously she began her dance, her hands moving in graceful, wave-like motions, then she quickened the pace, her movements melting into one another so quickly that the eye could scarcely follow them. She grasped the swords ; the glittering blades flashed and flickered and seemed to move round one another like serpents. Faster and faster she went; she was like a blurred whirlwind spun out of the silver thread of the swords. Her feet no longer seemed to touch the floor. She rushed towards the door, flew out with the speed of a swooping falcon, one stroke, and a pear tree, as thick as a man's arm, fell to the ground. The onlookers were astounded. In a second she was back in the room, stamped on the floor, and stood motionless as a statue, the swords pressed close to her sides.

Followed by her attendants, she withdrew. She was not out of breath, or hot; every hair was in place. About that time eight chests of tribute gifts had arrived from Eastern Turkistan. The Emperor gave orders that Hsiang Fei should take whatever she wanted; they were things from her own country.

For the sake of Hsiang Fei, the Emperor forgot his duties, among them that of honouring his mother. When days passed without his visiting her, she pretended that she was ill. Then he went. She warned him earnestly against the ungrateful Mohammedan prisoner of war and begged him to send her home to Aksu. The Emperor's reply was evasive.

Sad and depressed at Hsiang Fei's unbending hardness and her icy coldness, the Emperor endeavoured to break away from the net of bewitchment in which he was entangled, but he could think of nothing else, and, time after time, he returned to her apartment. Generally he stayed only a little while, watching her in silence, while she never even glanced in his direction. The ladies of her suite and her eunuchs begged her to submit to the Emperor's desires. He loved her. They warned her of his wrath if she persisted in her resistance; he might kill her. She made no answer. To escape from their importunities she drew a dagger and thrust it towards her throat. Terrified, her ladies rushed up and wrenched the dagger from her. "How dare you?" she cried. "Have I not many daggers? If you press me too hard I will take my own life. If the Emperor does not leave me in peace, I have a dagger that will serve for both of us."

This was looked upon as a direct threat against the Emperor's life and was reported to the chief eunuch. In turn he conveyed her words to the Empress, Fu-Ch'ai, who was both furious and terrified. But the relations between her and the Emperor had cooled; she dared not talk to him and warn him against Hsiang Fei. So she turned to the Empress-mother, Niuhulu, who was thoroughly conversant with the peculiarities of her favourite son. She knew that it would be worse than useless to warn him of danger and that the only thing to do was to put out the fire beneath the boiling pot. The two Empresses put their heads together.

In the meantime, Ch'ien-lung continued his visits to Hsiang Fei, but did not succeed in moving her in the very least. In his presence she was still silent and cold. He suffered agonies from the torment of his desire. The palace swarmed with the most beautiful women—he never even saw them. The most delicious dishes were placed before him—he did not touch them.

He was worried and troubled; he grew melancholy and morose; he grew thin and ill. "Here I sit, the ruler of the world," he thought, "yet I cannot win this loveliness. Our fate is decided by our previous lives. How can I possibly resist her? Use force—no—I cannot bring myself to do that."

The Empress-mother was deeply troubled. She must save her son. Upon his life depended the welfare of the whole empire and the future of the dynasty. She made her plans.

The winter solstice was approaching, and with it the day when the Emperor must offer up the great Sacrifice to Heaven. For three days beforehand he must bathe and fast in the Palace of Continence. On the day of sacrifice all the military and civil officials must be at the Altar of Heaven to receive the Emperor. Throughout this sacred rite, in the interests of the empire and the people, the Emperor could not escape for a moment from the thought of Hsiang Fei —"Four, five days have passed without my seeing her. Has she changed? What does she look like?"

When the sacrifice had been performed he hurried back to the Palace. All was still and dead. Hsiang Fei and all her retinue had vanished. In her apartment was nothing but disorder. Something had happened. The Emperor was seized by terrible suspicions. A eunuch bowed to the ground before him and told him that Hsiang Fei and her attendants had been summoned by the Empress. Beside himself with rage, the Emperor stamped on the floor, and hurried to the Kun-ming Palace.

His mother, the old Empress, had waited till her son was occupied with the Sacrifice to Heaven, then she had sent one of the eunuchs to summon Hsiang Fei and her retinue to wait upon her. She questioned the court ladies about Hsiang Fei's behaviour towards the Emperor. How often had he visited her ? What did they talk about ? What did Hsiang Fei busy herself with, and what did she say ? Had the Emperor spent nights with her ? Had the concubine shown gratitude or aversion ?

Then she made the ladies-in-waiting step aside, and Hsiang Fei came forward. All present were astounded at her unearthly beauty. The Empress-mother turned to Ch'ien-lung's wife and said : " A fascinating devil ! No wonder she has bewitched the Emperor ! "

Hsiang Fei did not fall to her knees. Proud and upright, she stood before the autocrat's mother. The Empress said : " Ever since you came to the Palace, His Majesty has treated you with the greatest favour. Are you grateful for this ? "

" Grateful ? Why ? " asked Hsiang Fei, coldly. " I hate him."

" Why do you hate His Majesty ? " asked the old Empress.

" I was happy with my husband in our Mohammedan country. Why did the Emperor send an army to take away our land, and why did he let them kill my lord ?

And, as if that were not enough, he had me brought to Peking. If only he had let me exercise the right of a prisoner of war, and kill myself! No, he had me brought to his palace. And even that was not all. He has constantly pursued me with his protestations of love."

Her forehead was wrinkled in a frown, her eyes flamed, and her cheeks burnt.

Superbly proud and filled with contempt for that cringing court, the Turkish woman towered above all the others, those who would destroy her because she alone among all creatures was master of the Ruler of the World.

The Empresses smiled at the tale of Ch'ien-lung's declarations of love. The old one then asked:

"What do you want most of all?"

Hsiang Fei answered:

"That your Majesty should grant me the favour of sending me home, so that I could rouse our armies to march against Peking and avenge my husband's death."

With an impatient gesture of her hand, the Empress-mother thrust aside such a thought.

"Be done with such figments of the brain, and do not dream of impossibilities."

"Then keep me in the palace until I get an opportunity to stab the Emperor, and thus secure vengeance."

Pale and furious, the Empress cried:

"Miserable slave! What has the Emperor ever done to you that you should behave like a criminal towards him?"

But she was interrupted by the Empress-mother who said :

" Let us hear her complaints to the end."

" Then I pray your Majesty to give me the favour of death without my body being mutilated. Let me go from this world with my chastity unstained."

Weeping, she threw herself to the floor, and repeated her prayer, time after time.

Touched, the Empress-mother said :

" The poor child, she is really to be pitied. We grant her prayer."

She commanded the chief eunuch to raise her up and conduct her to a side room, near Yüeh-hua-men (The Moon-Flower Gate), and there let her have her wish by strangulation.

Filled with gratitude, Hsiang Fei kotowed three times and followed the eunuch, while her ladies-in-waiting and serving women wept.

That was the day before the sacrifices were ended. Now the Emperor hurried home. He came too late. When he entered his mother's presence, he had first to perform the usual ceremonies and give an account of the sacrifices. Then he asked after Hsiang Fei. The Empress took his hand and said, comfortingly :

" That Mohammedan woman carried poison in her heart. If I had not got rid of her, a misfortune would have happened ; and if I had not prevented it how could I have stepped into the presence of your Ancestors' spirits ? Now the Mohammedan is dead, and you are free. Watch over your heart and your health that she has ruined."

She stroked his cheek. Stern, implacable etiquette forbade him to utter one word of reproach to his mother, or even a complaint. In silence he rose, bowed, and went out.

He ordered a eunuch to show him the place where Hsiang Fei's body was. She lay in a coffin made by her Mohammedans. Broken with sorrow, the Emperor reeled into the room. At the sight of Hsiang Fei he stopped as if turned to stone. Never had he seen her more lovely. The colour had not fled from her cheeks, she was scarcely cold. She seemed to be resting in endless peace after the superhuman struggle she had waged with such indomitable courage, and she smiled in her sleep over the victory she had won—a lovely Turkish woman stolen from Aksu who had stood with pride and steadfastness before the Emperor and the Court of the mightiest empire in the world. Overpowered by her celestial beauty and purity, the Emperor burst into floods of tears and putting his arms round her for the first time, he sobbed :

"It was I who killed you. Can you forgive me ?"

Then he mastered his emotion, rose in all his majesty and gazed at her steadfastly ; he stroked her hair, passed his fingers over her cheeks, and closed her eyes. Finally he drew a ring from her finger, whispering : "Farewell for ever, Hsiang Fei !" and hurried out to face the hard reality and cruel loneliness which, for long years, awaited him upon his Golden Dragon Throne.

But at Tung-ling, where the great Manchu Emperors are buried, a simple tombstone has stood for one hundred and seventy years outside the mausoleum of the Emperor Ch'ien-lung. There the summer winds rustle sadly above the grave of Hsiang Fei.

CHAPTER XI

HO SHÊN,[1] AN EMPEROR'S FAVOURITE

AMONG the Emperor Yung-chêng's famous women there was a Chinese, Ma Chia, who wore Manchu costume and surpassed all the others in beauty.

Prince Pao, afterwards the Emperor Ch'ien-lung, was the darling of all the court ladies. Only the proud Ma Chia treated him with coldness ; and as a result he was especially attracted by her. Unobserved and unannounced he used to creep to her apartment, tease her, and make her angry by kissing away the paint from her lips.

One day, when ladies-in-waiting were arranging her waving black hair, the Prince slipped into the room. The young girls prepared to greet him, but he made a sign for them to be silent, crept silently up to the back of her chair and put his hands over her eyes. Startled, she asked who it was. The Prince was silent. Ma Chia tried to free herself from the unknown by striking upwards with the ivory comb she had in her hand. The blow struck the prince on the forehead and he began to bleed. He loosed her and, with his hands pressed over the wound, hurried out. Ma Chia was in despair.

[1] Pl. XLVII.

The next day, the first of the month, when, according to Court etiquette, the princes and princesses must wait upon their parents, the Empress Niuhulu noticed the prince's wound. Drawing him to her, she petted him, and asked who had done it. Evasion being impossible, he admitted that the concubine Ma Chia had struck him by mistake, during a game. The Empress hated the lovely Ma Chia. In a fury of rage she sent for her, had her whipped, and then ordered a eunuch to take her out and strangle her. The prince was present, but dared not defy etiquette or the laws of filial piety by interceding for the unhappy girl ; he had to follow his mother back to the palace. Then he rushed to the Yüeh-hua gate, where Ma Chia stood, the cord round her neck, already half strangled.

Weeping, the prince exclaimed : " It is I who am guilty of your death."

Then he bit his finger, and let a drop of blood fall upon the girl's neck, with the words : " In this life I can do nothing for you, but come back to me in your next existence. Then with my life I will show you my gratitude. As a sign of recognition you shall bear this red spot on your neck."

With eyes brimming with tears Ma Chia died.

The prince bade her ladies give him the clothes she had worn, and spread them out on his bed. When he succeeded to the Dragon Throne, he had other things to think about, and the memory of Ma Chia's death gradually faded.

One day Ch'ien-lung had decided to go in his palanquin outside the walls of the Forbidden City. Before him were borne all the Imperial emblems, but the bearer of the umbrella-shaped shield of honour was missing. A dreadful happening. The Emperor was already sitting in his palanquin. Suddenly, one of the youths upon whose shoulders the poles rested, fell on his face before the Emperor and said: " The acting chief of the guard is to blame ! "

Unused to such familiarity from one of his lowest servants, the astonished Emperor ordered the youth to show his face. When he saw it, the Emperor seemed more astonished than ever, and stared at the youth in silence. He had seen that face before, but where, and when ? After sitting for some time lost in thought, he stepped out of the palanquin and went across to the palace library, ordering the youth to follow him. A eunuch took the trembling young man to the library, where the Emperor walked to and fro while the lowly bearer lay motionless on his face, awaiting sentence of death.

" What is your name ? " asked Ch'ien-lung.

" Ho Shên," answered the youth, his forehead on the floor.

" How old are you ? "

" Twenty-four years."

" Where do you come from ? "

" I am a Manchu."

Like a flash of lightning a thought struck the

Emperor; this youth was exactly like the unhappy concubine Ma Chia.

He felt his heart contract as the past rose up in his memory. He sat down in a chair, called the youth to him and ordered him to open the neck of his tunic.

The Emperor almost swooned when he saw a blood-red mark on the palanquin-bearer's neck. He could not control himself, but drew Ho Shên towards him, embraced him, and asked, tearfully:

"Tell me, why have you returned in the semblance of a man?"

Ho Shên thought the Emperor had gone mad and dared neither answer nor move; but he had time enough to assume the rôle that, within a short time, was to make him the mightiest man in China, mightier even than the Emperor himself. The Emperor told him the tragic story of Ma Chia. Weeping, Ho Shên whispered, modestly:

"Your Majesty has laid a great responsibility upon me."

Afterwards they talked together for a long time. The Emperor wished to repair the mistake of his youth which had caused the death of Ma Chia, and Ho Shên felt more and more assured, till he realized that he had the game in his own hands. When they parted, Ho Shên was a Marshal of the Imperial Household and the owner of 50,000 taels, costly objects of art, and fine robes of office.

Ho Shên rose in rank and became more and more indispensable to the Emperor. He possessed a boundless magic power over the Autocrat, who treated the former palanquin-bearer as if he were the newly incarnated Ma Chia. He loved Ho Shên till the day of his death.

When the court and the high officials saw the rising power of the favourite, they competed with one another to win his favour, flattered him, cringed to him, gave him money, property, lovely women, horses, jewels, pearls, and works of art.

Ho Shên was a wise man, but this boundless power went to his head and he misused his high office. He broke the law in all sorts of ways, and his avarice knew no bounds. His splendid palace, filled with the treasures of the whole world, swarmed with slaves and slave-girls, dancers and singers. Those who wished to be in favour with him bribed his servants to say a good word for them to their master. Ho Shên was the only one to whose advice the Emperor listened. Three-tenths of all the taxes of the country fell to the lot of Ho Shên, and in addition to this, he had already abstracted half the tribute from all the Chinese provinces and vassal states, for the collection of taxes passed through his hands. In his palace he had more precious works of art than the Emperor himself.

Not content with appropriating state property, when Ho Shên visited high officials, he had only to point to some valuable piece that pleased him, and it was his. At last people hid their valuables when they expected him to visit them.

His licentiousness aroused the anger of the censors, and accusations showered upon him, but to the Emperor he was always Ma Chia, and Ch'ien-lung seemed to believe that his fortunes were, in some mysterious way, tied up with that of Ho Shên.

The favourite climbed to still greater heights. He was made Chief Secretary of the Privy Council, and Imperial Chancellor. In his former capacity he had Liu Wên-chêng as his colleague. Liu had been ordered by the Emperor to keep a strict watch upon Ho Shên. He was a plain-spoken man who told the favourite just what he thought of his abuse of his power; but the Emperor always took Ho Shên's part. When Liu Wên-chêng returned home after subduing the Dzungars the Emperor sought to give the credit of the victory to Ho Shên, because the latter had helped to work out the plans for the campaign, and he gave him the title of Duke. This elevation encouraged Ho Shên to give a feast of rejoicing that lasted for seven days.

The Emperor graciously agreed to attend the first day's feast, and, in the evening, he set out to the favourite's palace. The whole length of the road from the Imperial Palace to the residence of the Imperial Chancellor was illuminated with lanterns: it looked as if a fiery dragon were creeping through the streets. Torches burnt everywhere: nothing so splendid had ever before been seen in Peking. Vast tent-roofs covered the courtyards and thick brocade mats were spread on the ground. When the Emperor drove to the great feast there was no sound from the horses' feet or the wheels of his carriage ; he might have imagined himself driving over a meadow.

Ho Shên met his exalted guest at the gateway. The President of the Ministry of Rites led the festivities ; the Commandant of Peking beat the kettle-drums in the Drum Tower, and the music was played by high officials.

The Emperor opened the feast. To the surprise of everyone he had chosen for the play of the evening a piece that dealt with the mythical Emperor Yao's abdication of the throne. He jested and talked with Ho Shên, who unceasingly encouraged him to drink. When his Majesty was intoxicated, the officials and ministers withdrew. Then Ho Shên sent for his slave dancers. They danced and sang, and more and more wine was drunk. Ho Shên ordered the most beautiful one to escort the Emperor to rest ; then Ch'ien-lung threw off his Imperial Robes, put on the dress of one of the Chinese actors, and asked the dancer :

" Do I not look precisely like a Chinese ? "

The drunken Ho Shên put on the Imperial robes, and asked :

" Do I not look precisely like your Majesty ? "

Dawn broke. As the Emperor rose, he noticed, on the inside of Ho Shên's tunic, a gold-embroidered dragon. He asked what it meant, and Ho Shên answered :

" This neck has been touched by your Majesty's

hand; in order to protect it I bear the Golden Dragon on my collar."

Then the Emperor touched the red mark on his favourite's neck and said:

"Yes, perhaps it is a premonition that you wear a Golden Dragon."

With superstitious care the Emperor cherished his favourite. Not only in matters of state and questions of war or peace was Ho Shên all-powerful, but even in small matters Ch'ien-lung took his advice. It was to Ho Shên that he turned when he was seized with a desire to enlarge and beautify the palace in Jehol that had been built by his exalted grandfather, K'ang-hsi. Just as K'ang-hsi had built thirty-six 'beautiful places' within the walls of the Summer Palace, so Ch'ien-lung would build thirty-six new 'beauty spots', and Ho Shên was commissioned to see that the work was done.

Ho Shên got together great numbers of workpeople, and within a few months had completed his task. Modelled after those in South China, so beloved of the Emperor, he had built on the slopes of "The Mountain of the Ringing Hammers", in groves of luxuriant trees, kiosks and summer-houses which peeped coquettishly from among the foliage. When the wind blew through the trees there was a rushing as of a waterfall. Under an arch of thick greenery through which not a gleam of sun could penetrate, the Emperor enjoyed the coolness and shade when the summer heat was at its height. The Emperor with his own hand wrote the inscriptions for these fairy places: " The Pine Tree Waves of the Ten Thousand Valleys ". A path wound down to a little lake surrounded by hills, pagodas, and kiosks, which were mirrored in the bright surface. In the lake was a low island protected by an embankment upon which grew rows of peach and willow trees hiding the mysterious pavilions whose rooms were lighted at night by lamps and torches. From them came the most bewitching music, and the sweetest singing—one knew that it was " The Island of the Blest ". Along the shores were pleasure pavilions, under whose eaves one could sit and watch the cooling showers of the rainy season. From a pagoda in the eastern part of the park the Emperor used to watch the lotus flowers and enjoy their perfume, borne on the wind. A waterfall fell over artificial cliffs, to split up into a thousand pearls in the mirror-like surface of the lake, and under the trees leapt magnificent harts.

On the top of a hill rose a red wall over-shadowed by ancient trees, behind which was a temple, " The Empress of the Many-Coloured Clouds ", and there the court ladies had to offer up incense. The Emperor often spent the night there so that he could enjoy the sunrise the next morning, and talk with Ho Shên and other members of his court.

At the foot of the hill there was a magnificent library with the finest collection of literature in the world. It exists to this day, unfortunately only in manuscript. In front of the library there was a terrace, surrounded by sweet-smelling plants, where the Emperor used to enjoy the moonlight in the autumn.

Ch'ien-lung would often surround himself with young people, especially onc of the princesses, his fifteenth son, Ho Shên's son, Têng-shên-ying-tê, and a daughter of the famous Chi Hsiao-lan, who all used to play together.

One autumn day, from the library terrace, Ch'ien-lung saw some harts grazing at the edge of the park. He wished to test the sureness of his son's aim and bade him shoot a hart in the head. The very first shot reached its mark. The Emperor was delighted and gave the prince a gold-mounted saddle as a reward. Then Ho Shên's son fell to his knees and begged the Emperor to allow him to show his skill : he would hit a hart in the eye. The Emperor willingly granted his request, and promised him the princess in marriage if he should succeed. Ho Shên was delighted at the possibility of his son's becoming the Emperor's son-in-law, and trembled with anxiety. He sank to his knees and thanked the Emperor for his gracious promise.

The boy took aim, drew the bow with a steady hand, and loosed the arrow. A hart fell and was brought to the Emperor. The arrow was embedded in the pupil of its eye. Wild jubilation broke out round the boy, who fell shyly on his knees before the Emperor. Even the Imperial Prince, who, in the future, under the name Chia-ch'ing, was to be Ch'ien-lung's successor, joined in the congratulations, and no one noticed the look of hatred and jealousy he shot at his fellow-competitor, who was also to be his brother-in-law. His hate embraced his rival's father too, Ho Shên, that man of common birth who ruled over the Emperor. At that moment he did not divulge his real feelings: the atmosphere of the court, laden with a thousand intrigues, had taught him patience and the art of dissimulation; but the day was to come when, as Emperor, he should take his revenge and send both Ho Shên and his son the yellow silken cord.

Ho Shên was no figure of fiction. During the latter part of Ch'ien-lung's reign he was the most powerful man in China. Even if, as the Chinese tales maintain, he did misuse his power, he must have been a wise and clever man, and, in addition to that, as his last days testify, a strong and inflexible character.

In Sir George Staunton's description of Lord Macartney's embassy from the King of England to the Emperor of China in 1793, we catch a passing glimpse of Ho Shên. There he is called Ho-choong-taung, Ho being the name, and the two following syllables his title. Staunton also gives him the title 'The Great Colao' or Prime Minister.

Upon the arrival of the embassy at Jehol, Lord Macartney was waited upon by two high officials, of whom one brought the compliments of the Emperor and the other those of Ho Shên. Of the favourite, Staunton says:

"The Vizier of China, who enjoyed almost exclusively the confidence of the Emperor, was said to be a Tartar of obscure birth and raised from an inferior station about twenty years before, when, while he was upon guard at one of the Palace gates, the Emperor passing through it, was struck merely with the comeliness of his countenance; but, afterwards, finding him to be a man of talent and education, he quickly elevated him to dignity; and he might be said to possess, in fact, under the Emperor, the whole power of the Empire."[1]

He adds that the Emperor shared the cares of that enormous kingdom with Ho Shên rather than trust him with the whole responsibility, and that he did not blindly follow all his advice.

"The manners of Ho-choong-taung were not less pleasing than his understanding was penetrating and acute. He seemed indeed to possess the qualities of a consummate statesman. . . . A daughter of the Emperor is married to a son of Ho-choong-taung. This circumstance was thought sufficient to alarm some of the imperial family, and other loyal subjects of the empire, as if they were fearful of the heights to which the ambition of that favourite might aspire. One man, indiscreetly zealous, undertook to present a memorial to his Imperial Majesty, exhorting him to declare his successor, as a measure of safety, to prevent future dissentions in the empire."[2]

The Englishmen were extremely surprised when, after the Emperor had given orders for them to be shown the Palace Park with all its wonderful beauties, the Prime Minister himself was instructed to be their guide.

[1] *An Authentic Account of an Embassy from the King of Great Britain to the Emperor of China* (London, 1797), Vol. 2, p. 210.

[2] Op. cit., Vol. 2, pp. 222–3.

> "The Great Vizier of the Empire, he whom the people almost considered as a second Emperor, was now ordered to give up some portion of his time from the calls and cares of government, to keep a stranger company in a mere tour of pleasure and curiosity."[1]

Staunton commends the attentiveness, the politeness and courtly manners with which Ho Shên conducted the Emperor's guests round the palaces, pavilions, kiosks, pagodas, and temples of Jehol.

Backhouse and Bland show how the Emperor's high ideals and wise rule, built up on a foundation of upright veneration for Heaven and for the spirits of his Ancestors, were counteracted and undermined by the Minister of State, Ho Shên, who introduced corruption into the highest positions, a fact which finally shook the foundations of the ancient kingdom. The Chinese historical judgment of Ho Shên is as follows: "An era of virtuous rule was brought to nought by Ho Shên; and the century of devastating insurrection and ruin that followed was his work and his alone."

The old, simple manner of living at the Manchu court was undermined by the example of frivolity and luxury set by the Grand Vizier. By his nepotism and corruption he sowed the seeds of all the rebellion that broke out during the reign of Chia-ch'ing.

But Ch'ien-lung shut his eyes and allowed Ho Shên to exercise despotic power under the very shadow of the throne. During the last ten years of

[1] Op. cit., Vol. 2, p. 240.

Ch'ien-lung's life all the reins of government of the kingdom were in the hands of Ho Shên. In all the provinces he had his tools. After the Emperor abdicated, in 1796, so that he should not disturb the spirit of his exalted grandfather by exceeding him in the length of his reign, the power of the favourite increased to the utmost, and his wealth assumed dimensions never before heard of in China. Thereby he aroused mistrust and jealousy and, when at last he met the usual fate of Emperor's favourites, when his protector was removed, he left possessions and treasures worth nine hundred million taels.

In the Biographical Sketches of the Ch'ing Dynasty (Ch'ing-shih-lieh-chuan, the 17th year of the Republic, 1928, part 35, pp. 1–9A) we find the biography of Ho Shên based on official documents. Professor F. Lessing, who has been kind enough to look through this biography for me, tells me that it is characterized by an incredible dryness. It contents itself with recording in chronological order all the data from this unusual man's official career, together with all the most important Imperial edicts. But from that register we can get a glimpse of the ups and downs of the career of the Emperor's favourite, and all the dangerous hidden rocks past which he had to steer his vessel. It looks as if, in his relations with Ho Shên, the Emperor had been stricken with blindness. Time after time he forgave him magnanimously and, if he had to punish him for some too glaring neglect of duty, he hastened to console him by loading him with new offices.

Ho Shên's glittering career began in Ch'ien-lung's thirty-fourth year (1769) and came to an end with the death of the Emperor. Almost half the biography is taken up by the Emperor Chia-Ch'ing's accusatory decrees against him.

The new Emperor hated the favourite, whose fate was sealed from the very first of the decrees in this long-drawn-out accusation.

A short summary of the proceedings will be sufficient :

1. The 1. i. 9. iv. Chia-ch'ing gave orders that there should be an investigation of Ho Shên's properties in Jehol.
2. On the same day an order was issued for an investigation of his burial-place at Chichou, to see whether he had overstepped the bounds set for persons of his rank.
3. A proclamation of the 19. i. iv. Chia-ch'ing, concerning the sins of Ho Shên :

   A. As Ch'ien-lung in his 60th year had, by a special edict, named Chia-ch'ing his heir to the throne, Ho Shên betrayed the secret by publicly handing him a sceptre (*ju-i*).

   B. At an audience which Ch'ien-lung granted him in the old Summer Palace (Yüan-ming-yüan) he did not keep his right place, but rode straight into the inner court-yards.

C. On account of an injury to his leg, he had himself carried even into the palace.

4. He has taken one of the palace ladies as his concubine.
5. During one of the rebellions he arbitrarily withheld news from the front, or even utterly concealed news from his Emperor Ch'ien-lung.
6. During the illness of His Imperial Majesty he showed no grief, but jested and talked before and after audiences as if nothing were the matter.
7. When, during his illness last winter, the Emperor Ch'ien-lung once wrote illegible marginal notes on a rescript, Ho Shên dared to observe that it would be better to tear them off, and he himself drew up a new rescript.
8. When he was ordered by the Emperor Ch'ien-lung to assist the Ministers for the Interior, Justice, and Finance, he seized the whole power for himself and ruled in an arbitrary manner.
9. A petition to the throne of last December concerning plundering by robbers in Hsien-hua and Kuei-tê, when the Dalai Lama's merchants were robbed of their cattle and two persons were killed, he dismissed arbitrarily in that he suppressed the petition.
10. When We, after the death of our blessed father, issued a decree to the Mongol princes informing them that those who had not had

small-pox need not appear at festivities in Peking, he so altered it that it appeared that none were to come.

11. He gave ministerial posts to his private tutors.
12. The names of the candidates for the Privy Council were suppressed by him.
13. Upon investigation of his possessions it was discovered that he had overstepped the permitted boundaries, and that in decoration and ornamentation he had, in many respects, copied the Ning-shou Palace. His courtyards differed no whit from those on the Island of the Blest beside the Terrace of Fairies in the Summer Palace in Jehol. What can have been his intentions ?
14. Another complaint about the dimensions of the mausoleum.
15. His pearls and valuables are far in excess of the court jewels. In his possession he has one pearl that is larger than the one in Our crown.
16. It is the same with other precious stones.
17. He has in his possession silver to the value of several million.
18. In the space between his walls he has hidden 26,000 taels of silver. In his secret treasure chamber over 6,000 taels in gold, and in the cellar over a million in silver.
19. In the neighbourhood of Peking, in T'ung-chou and Chi-chou, he has kept pawn shops and

money exchanges with a capital of 100,000 taels, a trade that is not fitting for a Chancellor.

20. A certain Lui Ch'uan, a member of his household who is merely a slave, has a fortune of 200,000 taels which could not have been amassed except by dishonest means.

More and more complaints poured down on the head of the Chancellor, who up to now had been all-powerful. He was accused of having detailed from the regular Army over a thousand men as guards and servants for his palaces, and of having maintained them out of public money.

On the 27. 2. IV. Chai-ch'ing issued an edict saying that among Ho Shên's possessions had been found an imperial chain of ceremony, of real pearls, an object that, in no circumstances, might any subject, however highly placed, possess. According to the Chancellor's household, Ho Shên was in the habit of putting it round his neck in the evening, when the lamps were lit, and of standing before a mirror and talking to himself, and smiling at his reflection. He spoke so low that they had never been able to hear what he was saying. Had this been known before Ho Shên's death he would have been doomed to execution in one form or another. But, on the 18th of the 1st month, the Emperor had decided to send him the yellow silk cord, which would oblige him to take his life.

After the doom had fallen, Ho Shên kotowed

towards the Imperial Palace, thanked His Majesty for his clemency and said to his son :

" We two have served our old master together. It is in accordance with ancient practice that a Minister should follow his lord to the Nine Springs. I shall attend His Sainted Majesty as of old, and receive his wise counsel. The present Emperor has loyal servants about him, and is well rid of men such as we are."

Having put the cord round his neck without assistance he said : " His late Majesty will feel indignant wrath in the Halls of Hades " and hanged himself.

The misdeeds of this remarkable man are redeemed to a great extent by the fact that, in spite of the most brutal torture and the cries of denunciation from his countless enemies, he remained proud and inflexible to the very end, readily admitted his mismanagement of public affairs and his enormous defalcations, and never once involved one of his fellow-scoundrels.

He did not even deny that he had hankered after the Imperial Dragons and desired the downfall of the dynasty that he had served for so many years ; the dynasty that, through his misdeeds, was doomed to disintegration, and, together with the Imperial power in China, was to die away in the night of time.

CHAPTER XII

CHIA-CH'ING'S DEATH IN JEHOL

As he required more room for his women's quarters, the Emperor Chia-ch'ing decided to build some new pavilions in the park of the Summer Palace in Jehol and sent an official to Hang-chou to buy wood. When the man returned, he brought with him a model of the Mirror Kiosk at Hsi-hu, ' The Western Lake ', which had been built by a certain Wang and his wife for the Governor-General. Having learnt that the Emperor was about to enlarge the palace at Jehol, the Governor had sent him the model and the two clever craftsmen with a letter recommending their skill and artistry to the Emperor.

The model had been packed in an elegant chest and it was taken out by the chief eunuch in the presence of His Majesty. The roof-tiles of the kiosk were of glass, the column of crystal, and the walls inset with thousands of tiny mirrors that broke up the light in all directions. In the middle was a beautiful ivory bed.

The Emperor was delighted with this work of art, and immediately sent for Wang and his wife. As they could not appear before him unless they had some official status, he bestowed upon them the button of the 7th rank.

Dressed in the clothes belonging to their new rank, the two Wangs appeared before the Emperor and kotowed, their faces to the ground. Wang Sên, the craftsman, shook with fear in the presence of the Son of Heaven, but his wife knelt beside her husband, her head lowered, perfectly calm. Her unusual beauty and the whiteness of her skin made a deep impression on Chia-ch'ing, and he ordered her to look up. Her eyebrows were two fine arches which almost reached the dark hair beside her temples, and the red on her cheeks glowed against the white skin. Her beauty far surpassed that of all the young women in the Emperor's Palace.

Smiling, he asked her her maiden name.

"Tung," she answered, shyly.

"How long have you been married?"

"Four years."

"Did you help your husband to make this model?"

"He made the tiles, columns, and walls, I did the wood carving and the fine work in the interior," she answered.

"In truth you are a gifted pair," the Emperor said, and he gave orders that Wang Sên should be attached to the Bureau of Imperial Craftsmen, pending preferment, and that his wife was to join the Chinese ladies who were attached to the palace in various artistic capacities.

Wang's wife was given no special work to do but she had to attend the Emperor daily on the 'Island of the Blest' (Chiung-tao-ch'un-yin). Nothing could have been more abhorrent to her, but she knew that it would be useless to protest. Soon she realized that the Emperor was a gentle, good-natured man, and she ventured to ask him if she might see her husband again. He merely smiled, and said :

"Wait for one year, and I will send you home. You have seen Hsi-hu ?"

"The 'Western Lake' is my home ; how could I help seeing it ?"

Then the Emperor ordered her to make a model of Hsi-hu and the surrounding country. She made it in clay while the Emperor watched her, mixed her colours, and baked the clay. Quietly they worked side by side like any other happy pair. From time to time, overcome by his emotion, the Emperor would have drawn her into his arms, but she resisted, saying, with tears in her eyes :

"Your Majesty, three thousand beauties stand at your beck and call. Why will you steal from me my virtue as a wife ?"

Then the Emperor was touched, and let her alone. But she had become essential to him ; the time he spent on the 'Island of the Blest', talking and jesting with Wang's wife, had become a part of his daily life.

Once he said to her :

"Even in olden times beautiful women were

beyond count, but I wonder if any one of them could have made me forget both food and sleep, as you have done."

In the flowery quarters, the women soon learnt of the Emperor's infatuation for the young southerner, and she became the object of bitter jealousy. When they saw with what irresistible power Wang's wife drew the Emperor to the 'Island of the Blest' the rumour began to go round that she was a fox-demon who had bewitched him. This rumour reached even the ears of the faithful, virtuous Empress, who did her best to calm the concubines. Perhaps she knew that there was no cause for jealousy, as, despite her great beauty, Wang's wife always kept the Emperor at a chaste distance and never allowed any familiarities. The Emperor respected her and allowed it to be as she wished. At the very most he might occasionally press her hand lovingly.

During this time Wang Sên felt lonely and deserted, where he was installed with the Imperial handicraft-workers. He thought continually of his lovely wife and constantly begged the eunuchs to arrange a meeting, but they dared not. Gradually Wang Sên grew gloomy and strange, and seemed almost to be losing his mind; first he cried, then he laughed or sang, and for hours he would sit, staring into the distance, sunk in thought. His companions no longer bothered about him.

One day Wang met the Emperor coming out of the Palace. He threw himself on his face and begged that his wife might be given her freedom. But the Emperor only smiled and said:

"Your wife is such a skilful painter that the Empress desires to keep her. I will give you a palace girl to keep you company when you are lonely."

That evening Wang found a girl in his quarters and a room had been prepared for them, but, though they remained together for three nights, Wang Sên was not unfaithful to his wife.

Wang Sên's sickness of spirit increased; he cried and lamented, and all the time called out his wife's name. When this came to the ears of the Emperor, he raised Wang Sên to the 5th rank, gave him 20,000 taels, and sent him back to the south. The palace girl, who was also from the south, went with him. She was sincerely fond of him, and would willingly have become his wife, but Wang said:

"My wife and I love one another very dearly, even if she now belongs to the Palace and is kept away from me. I will never be unfaithful to her."

He gave the girl 3,000 taels and sent her home to her parents, but he himself returned secretly to Jehol. When he arrived there he gave a eunuch an enormous bribe to bring him news of his wife.

The eunuch was sorry for the poor simple fellow and went off to the palace to see what he could find out. After two days he returned to Wang Sên with a letter in which she said that, although the Emperor loved her passionately, she had remained faithful to him during ten long months. She had implored the

Emperor to allow her to return after the expiration of a year . . . now they would soon be together again.

This message rejoiced Wang beyond all measure. Now he waited quite calmly for the great day to come. He would often spend joyous hours with the eunuch in tea-houses or wine-shops, and the eunuch told him strange and mysterious tales of the life within the palace walls.

The nearer the happy day approached, the more anxious Wang Sên grew, till he was like a cat on hot bricks. He had arranged with the eunuch that he was to be found in the Lake Tower, which stood upon the shore of a small lake and had a wine-shop on an upper story. There he sat, anxiously waiting over his wine.

Suddenly the eunuch appeared. His face was drawn and haggard and Wang immediately feared that he bore bad news.

"What of my wife?" he asked, impatiently.

"Be calm! You know your wife has won the love of the Emperor: every day he kept her company while she was working and sent her dresses and ornaments. They often played chess together and laughed and jested. Two days ago he was detained in her apartment by a concubine who had quarrelled with your wife and it happened that she was left to work alone in her room. Yesterday a misfortune happened."

At these words Wang Sên turned pale as death. The eunuch tried to console him, then continued:

"Last night, when the night-watchman had struck the third watch he heard one of the palace doors creak. I myself heard the sound, half in a dream, but I went on sleeping. Afterwards I thought I heard the sound of a window opening, and it seemed to me that it was one of the windows in the 'Island of the Blest.' At the same instant I heard a woman's voice crying for help. I threw on my clothes and, with my room mates, hurried to the Island. The window of the room where your wife slept was open ; the bed was in disorder, and slippers and pins were scattered over the floor. A pin that your wife always wore lay on the verandah, and she had disappeared. Early in the morning I reported the matter to His Majesty, and he ordered us to search everywhere. On Lake T'ai-yeh we found a red veil floating, and, by the pattern and the embroidery, the Emperor knew that it was one of your wife's. Then he had the lake dragged, but it was in vain."

Wang Sên had listened to the eunuch's story, torn between hope and despair. When he saw that there was no more hope, with a wild cry of "My wife ! My poor unhappy wife !" he leapt to the window, and, before the eunuch could hinder him, had sprung into the lake.

In this way he was drowned, and joined his beloved wife at last.

This event made a profound impression on the ageing Emperor. During his last years, sad misfortunes had crowded round his throne and weighed down his spirits. He had grown weary of ruling the empire, and left everything to his chancellor, Mujangga, but Mujangga was false to his master, and only anxious to obtain as much as possible for himself. Unrest broke out on all sides, and bad news came thick and fast. The Emperor was only told what was considered good for him; Mujangga suppressed all bad news. The only faithful one was Prince Chih, and he had not the ear of the Emperor.

Then, too, the eternal quarrels among the concubines made life bitter for the old monarch, and fed anew his longing for the lovely and dexterous woman from the Western Lake.

At last he began to fail. Throughout his illness he was faithfully tended by Prince Chih, who took no rest day or night. For the seventy days during which the Emperor was fighting with death, Mujangga ruled supreme, and no one dared dispute his authority. Three months after his collapse, the Emperor Chia-ch'ing knew that the end was near, and summoned all the ministers, with Mujangga at their head, to his death-bed, and made known his will. It appeared that by a secret edict issued in the fourth year of his reign, he had appointed his eldest son Prince Chih (Prince Ming-ning) as his successor, and that this decree had been hidden behind the inscription above the Dragon Throne, "Right, Honesty, Splendour, Illumination". All were to obey him.

One night in the late summer of the year 1820, while the Emperor lay on his death-bed with only his favourite concubine on watch, a furious thunderstorm broke over Jehol and the hills surrounding the Summer Palace. Lightning flashed across the sky and the thunder rolled like the Day of Judgment. A thunderbolt fell upon the pavilion where the Emperor lay and in a second it was in flames. In the ashes two charred corpses were found, those of the Son of Heaven and his concubine.

The orthodox maintain that, by this death-blow, Heaven had announced its wrath against her Son because, only a week after his accession to the throne, in the midst of the deepest court mourning for the Emperor Ch'ien-lung, he had taken the life of Ho Shên, and dismissed from office all the dead Emperor's trusted servants.

Chapter XIII

HSIEN-FÊNG'S DEATH IN JEHOL

One more Emperor was to die in Jehol—Hsien-fêng. He was, if possible, a more feeble monarch than Chia-ch'ing who had ended his days in the Summer Palace in 1820. The events which led up to this melancholy chapter in the history of China were as follows : [1]

Yehonala was the daughter of a general in command of one of the Manchu Eight Banners ; she came of a famous Manchu family and lived with her parents in the Street of the Tinsmiths, in the eastern quarter of Peking. She was strikingly beautiful, intelligent, well read, clever, and ambitious.

Yung-lu, a youth of her own age, was her betrothed.

The Master of Ten Thousand Years, the Son of Heaven, the Emperor Tao-kuang, died in 1850, and was succeeded on the Dragon Throne by his dissipated and perverted son Hsien-fêng. It was the duty of the Dowager Empress to approve the bevy of beautiful girls who were destined to become the Emperor's concubines.

[1] Charles Pettit, *La femme qui commanda à cinq cent millions d'hommes* (Paris, 1928).

Yehonala was one of those who were approved and, at the age of eighteen, she was given the high rank of concubine of the third class. In accordance with the Rites, the chief eunuch An Tê-hai had to examine her and make sure that she was healthy, perfectly formed, and voluptuous. He fell in love with her, and it was not until some time had passed that she could prevail upon her impotent admirer to take her to the Emperor's bedchamber. The Emperor Hsien-fêng was childless and did not care about women, but her frank behaviour pleased him. In time she became pregnant and gave birth to a son. This promoted her to the rank of first concubine and as, at the same time, the Empress had the misfortune to bear a daughter, Yehonala's star was in the ascendant. The Emperor sank deeper and deeper into dissipation, and it was evident that the concubine's son would be his successor, and the concubine herself, Empress. Her influence increased. She distributed high titles to her kinsmen, and made her former lover, Yung-lu, commander of the Palace Guard. The Emperor's younger brother, the wise and temperate Prince Kung, ruled the kingdom as President of the Council. At that time China was tottering on the edge of the abyss; the T'ai-p'ing rebellion was raging and the Yangtse valley provinces were in the hands of the rebels.

In the midst of all this unrest, the court received dreadful news: the barbarians with the white faces were coming. In 1860, the English and French fleets under Lord Elgin and Baron Gros had arrived off the Taku Forts, but had been repulsed: the next year they were back again, lying off the mouth of the Pei-ho with 300 ships. The foreign troops landed and began their march to Peking. The imperial armies, the Tartar and Manchu cavalry were annihilated and the enemy reached the capital.

At that moment, when his empire was trembling in the balance and it was plainly his duty to stay at his post, the faint-hearted Emperor declared his intention of following ancient custom and going to Jehol for the autumn hunting. The favourite concubine, Yehonala, stormed at him, accused him of cowardice, and exhorted him not to leave the capital, but Hsien-fêng would not listen to her and set out with his following for Jehol. Then she called upon Prince Kung to try and save the dynasty. He was a brave man, and promised that he would stay in the Violet City as long as possible. Yehonala wished to remain in Peking, but Prince Kung pointed out that it was her duty to go with the Emperor to Jehol to try to prevent him from perpetrating any more disasters by his cowardice, and to watch over her son, the last hope of the dynasty.

She took his advice and hastened after the Imperial procession. It had just left the first halting-place, the Summer Palace (Yüan-ming-yüan) twenty *li* to the north of the Tartar City, a fairy palace crowded with the richest collection of art treasures in the whole world. In that brilliant procession of palanquins, carriages, troops, and pack animals, she found her son with her rival the Empress, a woman who set the dynasty before any personal feelings.

There was the wildest confusion on the road to Jehol, for countless refugees were following the example of the fleeing Emperor. Slowly, the heavily laden procession approached the summer residence of K'ang-hsi and Ch'ien-lung. It was twilight, and there seemed to be a strange light in the sky. Yehonala stepped out of her palanquin to see what it was. In the south the sky was flaming red. It was a gigantic fire. The Summer Palace (Yüan-ming-yüan) was burning. The French and English troops had reached Peking and set fire to the richest and most wonderful palace in the world. Inestimable treasures of art and literature were lost for ever. A base crime against humanity and good taste had been perpetrated. Is it surprising that the Chinese called them barbarians and foreign devils?

At last the Imperial procession reached Jehol. Yehonala kept in constant touch with Prince Kung, who, by his tact, diplomacy and dignity, had succeeded in saving Peking from the fate of the Summer Palace.

Here follows a somewhat romanticized account of the death of Hsien-fêng.

The Emperor had given to his concubine Yehonala the title Yi. During his stay in Jehol the Emperor's sickness, aggravated by his licentious life, increased, and during this time his suspicion that the energetic and domineering concubine would thrust out the rightful Empress, and, like the vigorous female rulers of the Han and T'ang Dynasties, seize all the power for herself, grew stronger and stronger. In order to avert such a danger to the throne he decided to have her put to death. He called the Empress and the Prime Minister Su-shun to his sick-bed and made known his decision, but the Empress interceded for her rival and the Emperor contented himself with adding an edict to his will, to the effect that the Yi concubine was to be put to death immediately her behaviour gave rise to any apprehension. This document, in which she was referred to as " an utterly untrustworthy person ", was countersigned by the Empress and Su-shun. The Empress advised the addition of Prince Kung's signature, and the Emperor summoned him to Jehol. The document was concealed beneath his pillow.

The Yi concubine had noticed the Emperor's increasing coldness towards her, and had ordered her trusty servants to find out what was going on. One of these had been listening at the window while the Emperor was consulting with his Empress and Su-shun, and when the conversation was reported to her, the Yi concubine realized that her life was in danger.

That night, to assuage his pain, and send him to sleep, the Emperor sent for Li Lien-ying to massage him. The eunuch was a wise and cunning man, the only person who could get the Emperor to sleep. When the Emperor dropped off, the eunuch saw the paper projecting from under the pillow, and his curiosity was increased when he read the words " an utterly untrustworthy person ". He studied the whole document most carefully.

Through his skill as a hairdresser and masseur, and his clever tales and tricks, Li Lien-ying had won the favour of the Yi concubine. Now he told her everything and warned her to be on her guard. After that she often took the little crown-prince on her arm and went to visit the sick-room to appeal to the heart of her child's father, and watch the rival Empress.

In the meantime Prince Kung had arrived from Peking to sign the document, although his sympathies were really with the concubine. He told Yung-lu, the Chief of the Palace Guard, the secret that was the subject of daily discussions between Su-shun and other high officials. Fearing the influential Yi concubine who, when the Emperor died, would be the Empress Mother and therefore the most powerful person in the land, they had decided to help another prince, Prince Yi, to seize the throne. But, before anything definite had been accomplished, the Emperor Hsien-fêng died in the Yen-po-chih-chuang apartments.

Su-shun immediately named himself Administrator of State Affairs and gave out that the Emperor had appointed Prince Yi his successor. He also announced that the Imperial Princes and high officials need not come to the mourning feast at Jehol, as it was his intention to remove the Emperor's body to Peking at once.

But the Yi concubine had forestalled him ; before the death of the Emperor she had abstracted the great seal, and when Su-shun inquired where it was, she said that Prince Kung had taken it with him to Peking. The Prime Minister decided to hurry to the capital and get possession of the seal.

The Yi concubine, who knew that she was playing a dangerous game, hastened to the Dowager Empress, the heir to the throne in her arms, and begged for her help. The Empress allowed herself to be persuaded to send a messenger with letters to the Princes Kung and Ch'un and the Commander of the Guard, the concubine's former lover, commanding them to place themselves at the disposal of the heir to the throne and his mother.

Su-shun wished to keep the two Empresses in Jehol while he escorted the Emperor's body to Peking, but both ladies insisted on going with the funeral cortège. Under the pretence of protecting them, but in reality in order that he could have the heir to the throne and his mother done to death on the road to the capital, Su-shun took with him a big escort.

Once again the far-sighted concubine had forestalled him. She had sent a message to her faithful lover Yung-lu, ordering him to hasten to Jehol with 4,000 men as a protection for the Emperor's funeral procession. At the gates of the Summer Palace, she was met by Yung-lu, whose men surrounded the two Empresses. When Su-shun, who rode with his men at the head of the procession, found that his plan had miscarried, he decided to hurry on to Peking, and issue a forged edict from the late Emperor, depriving the Yi concubine of all her honours, and appointing Prince Yi heir to the throne.

But the clever concubine had foreseen even this eventuality and now, exerting all her energies, she succeeding in reaching Peking ahead of the Prime Minister. She immediately called together the two Princes Kung and Ch'un and all her faithful followers, and when, as a proof of her power, she produced the great seal, everyone agreed, and it was decided that her son should mount the Dragon Throne under the title T'ung-chih.

The following day Prince Kung sent his troops to meet the funeral procession, while the rooms in the Palace were being decorated with lamps and hangings of the mourning colours so that the coffin should be fittingly received.

In Min-yün, where Su-shun was waiting with the Emperor's catafalque, he was surrounded by Prince Kung's troops and brought to Peking as a prisoner. Amid the jubilation of the populace he was publicly executed, and his head hung in a wicker cage for all to behold.

So the Yi concubine, the lovely Manchu girl, succeeded not only in crushing all opposition in Jehol and Peking, but climbed to the topmost pinnacle of power and ruled the empire for fifty years as the Dowager Empress Ts'u-hsi.

* * * * * *

Our days in Jehol were ended and it was time to return to Peking. For my part, the Manchu

Emperors' summer city had made a profound impression on me, an impression both sympathetic and melancholy, that city which in its heyday had been one of the greatest and most noble jewels in the Imperial Crown. A deep study and detailed description of the topography and orientation of all the many different temples and groups of buildings would have taken more time than we had at our disposal and would have been outside the scope of this book.

We wished above everything to return to Peking by boat down the Luan-ho, of whose beauty we had heard so much, but, not long before, there had been a foreign diplomat in Jehol, and his request to be allowed to return by river had been refused, on the score that the water level was too low. It was rumoured that Marshal Chang Hsüeh-liang had ordered the Governor, General Tang Yü-lin, to prevent the journey, as the boundary between Jehol and Hopei was said to be infested with bandits and the authorities could count on a very awkward situation if a foreign diplomat fell into their hands.

To be sure, we were not diplomats, but we feared that the same obstacles would be put in the way of our return by boat, so we had decided to try and trick the General by not mentioning how we proposed to go back to Peking. We had come in our own car and had used it every day in Jehol. Now, if we secretly hired a boat to wait for us on the shore of the Luan-ho, loaded our baggage on the car and drove out of the town, nobody would suspect that we were not going to take the usual road over Ku-pei-k'ou back to Peking.

But the General was craftier than we were. The night before our departure he sent a message to Father Mullie regretting that he could not see us off personally, but saying that there would be military honours, and that he had commanded an officer and ten soldiers to escort us on our journey down the river as far as the boundary of his province.

Jehol, City of Emperors! Since the Emperor Hsien-fêng ended his life in the Summer Palace, and the famous Yi concubine, mother of the Emperor T'ung-chih, left that place of memories in the land of the Harchin Mongols in 1861, its sun has sunk for ever.

But the memories of great happenings still hover about the stately temples and palaces. The Dzungar hordes pass like penitents, and the tattered banners of the Torgot flutter there. The trumpets and drums sound in the Tashi Lama's monastery-court, and, followed by glittering hosts, the descendants of Chinghis Khan ride the wild horses of the grassland beside the Jehol river. A never-ending array of splendidly clad figures from the greatest age of China passes by like ghosts, while, almost imperceptibly, the twilight folds its wings above the silent hills.

THE END

INDEX OF PERSONS

Index of Persons

INDEX OF PLACES

Index of Places